32 Virtual, Augmented,
and Mixed Reality Programs for Libraries

ALA Editions purchases fund advocacy, awareness, and accreditation programs for library professionals worldwide.

32 VIRTUAL, AUGMENTED, & MIXED REALITY

PROGRAMS FOR LIBRARIES

edited by **ELLYSSA KROSKI**

ALA
Editions
CHICAGO | 2021

ELLYSSA KROSKI is the director of Information Technology and Marketing at the New York Law Institute as well as an award-winning editor and author of sixty books including *Law Librarianship in the Age of AI* for which she won AALL's 2020 Joseph L. Andrews Legal Literature Award. She is a librarian, an adjunct faculty member at Drexel University and San Jose State University, and an international conference speaker. She received the 2017 Library Hi Tech Award from the ALA/LITA for her long-term contributions in the area of Library and Information Science technology and its application. She can be found at www.amazon.com/author/ellyssa.

© 2021 by the American Library Association

Extensive effort has gone into ensuring the reliability of the information in this book; however, the publisher makes no warranty, express or implied, with respect to the material contained herein.

ISBNs
978-0-8389-4948-1 (paper)

Library of Congress Cataloging-in-Publication Data

Names: Kroski, Ellyssa, editor.
Title: 32 virtual, augmented, and mixed reality programs for libraries / edited by Ellyssa Kroski.
Other titles: Thirty-two virtual, augmented, and mixed reality programs for libraries
Description: Chicago : ALA Editions, 2021. | Includes bibliographical references and index.
  | Summary: "Ranging from gaming activities utilizing VR headsets to augmented reality tours, exhibits, immersive experiences, and STEM educational programs, the program ideas in this guide include events for every size and type of academic, public, and school library" —Provided by publisher.
Identifiers: LCCN 2021004662 | ISBN 9780838949481 (paperback)
Subjects: LCSH: Virtual reality—Library applications—United States. | Libraries—Activity programs—United States.
Classification: LCC Z678.93.S53 A14 2021 | DDC 025.5/7006--dc23
LC record available at https://lccn.loc.gov/2021004662

Book design by Alejandra Diaz in the TisaPro, Korolev, and Atrament typefaces.

♾ This paper meets the requirements of ANSI/NISO Z39.48-1992 (Permanence of Paper).

Printed in the United States of America
25 24 23 22 21   5 4 3 2 1

Contents

Contents

Preface

Virtual, augmented, and mixed reality—VR, AR, and MR—technologies are currently being implemented in libraries to provide engaging programming events and educational opportunities. Libraries are enhancing their exhibits, collections, and lessons as well as providing virtual field trips to landmarks and art museums, driver safety programs, 3D coding environments, and even simulated space exploration. They are organizing workshops, establishing lending programs, and teaching patrons how to utilize their own VR equipment.

32 Virtual, Augmented and Mixed Reality Programs for Libraries is an all-in-one guide to how to plan, organize, and run all types of new and emerging virtual events in libraries. Programs range from simple gaming activities utilizing VR headsets to AR tours, exhibits, and immersive experiences, to STEM educational programs. Programs encompassing new technologies, such as AR, VR, and MR, are all included.

Each program walks the reader through step-by-step instructions on how to prepare for and host these events. Every program includes a materials and equipment list, a budget, and recommendations for age ranges and type of library. Programs range in cost, topic, and difficulty; so, there is something for every size and type of library. The authors who describe these programs are all knowledgeable professionals from the library field and offer real-world programming ideas for public, school, and academic libraries.

I heartily thank all the knowledgeable librarians and experts who contributed their time and expertise to this book. It was a pleasure to work with all of you.

Virtual Reality Is for Everybody
Connecting with Harder-to-Serve Populations

CHERYL MARTIN, Library Services Specialist

North Olympic Library System, Washington

Virtual reality in public libraries is closer to reality than you may think. With a few VR headsets, empathetic and well-trained staff, and an 8 × 8-foot space, you can bring VR to your library patrons. Teen and adult patrons of all ages and abilities can experience VR, from swimming with dolphins to climbing Mount Everest to walking on the moon with Neil Armstrong and everything in between.

The North Olympic Library System (NOLS) offered these and other programs to more than six hundred participants over a ten-month period using four Oculus VR headsets. Participants were aged thirteen and older, with most of the participants falling in the sixty-plus age range. Though several participants had physical and cognitive disabilities, with support and simple modifications, they were equally as able to enjoy the VR experience as those without such disabilities.

A variety of program types are possible and can include in-library, community outreach, and outreach to the homebound through themed programs or introductory, drop-in, or reserved sessions. Through a variety of program offerings, attention to accessibility issues, and a willingness to think outside the box, you can introduce VR to nearly everyone.

Age Range	Type of Library Best Suited For	Cost Estimate
Young adults (ages 13–18) Adults	Public libraries Academic libraries	$2,800–$3,400 ($3,800–$4,400 with optional equipment)

PROGRAM CONSIDERATIONS

This program is suggested for young adults ages thirteen through seventeen with parent permission and adults over eighteen of all ages and abilities. A signed health and safety release is recommended for all participants.

This cost estimate is based on purchasing four Oculus Quest and two Oculus Go headsets, plus the supporting equipment, applications, and consumable supplies. You can look to partnerships and technology grants to reduce program and equipment costs. Staff costs and desk chairs are not included in these estimates, which also do not include sales tax or shipping costs.

Figure 1.1   North Olympic Library System patrons, staff, and volunteers accessing VR experiences through the library

OVERVIEW

The Virtual Reality Experience

Many kinds of programs can be offered in and out of your library that can all be tailored to fit your library's unique needs. Individual session lengths can range from fifteen minutes to an hour. Complete sessions can be two to three hours without backup batteries, longer if using supplemental battery packs or by allowing for time between each session for headset recharging. How long each participant remains comfortable with their VR experience will vary. How frequently you can offer such programs will vary and depend on such resources as staffing and the space available.

It is important to ask how a participant is doing throughout their VR experience. Be observant and pay attention to body language and verbal cues to maximize a positive VR experience and ensure the safety of the participant, staff, and observers. Provide seating for observers and keep chairs close at hand for participants who may need to sit during the VR experience. You can keep a safe space around each VR participant by placing blue painter's tape on the floor to mark the player's boundaries to replicate that of the play space provided inside the user's headset.

It is important to recognize that participants may require extra assistance for several reasons. Older adults are usually willing and may be eager to try new technology, though some may still feel apprehensive or uncomfortable when they start. Adults with cognitive or physical limitations may not be able to use the equipment on their own. It is important to make sure you are communicating clearly with the participant, and if they have a caregiver, that they are present and assisting during the VR experience. The headset can be set in different languages. However, not all applications have foreign language options; so, keep this in mind. Your goal is to give the best VR experience you can while accommodating each participant's unique needs.

In-Library Programs

- *Drop-by events* are good for short, fifteen- to twenty-minute introductory VR experiences. While these events can work well for busier locations, they work best for low-volume and smaller branches with less demand.
- *Preregistered sessions* provide longer sessions for your participants that can be scheduled ahead. Such sessions work well with larger branches and high-demand locations and are preferred by returning participants.

- *Group events* are the perfect venue for students and small community groups. The NOLS examples provided include a group of Japanese exchange students and their host students, members of a local Chamber of Commerce, and a group of disabled adults from a local residence home.
- *Themed registered events* offer sessions centered around a particular VR application for patrons who register ahead. NOLS examples include an Apollo 11 VR experience, Guided Meditation, and Ocean Rift. Nearly any application can be adapted to a themed event.
- *In-library experiences* allow patrons to check out Oculus Go headsets.

Community Outreach

Your events can be drop-in, preregistered, and/or themed, similar to in-library experiences. Some suggested community partners include senior centers, assisted living facilities, local Chamber of Commerce members, community centers, Upward Bound, and other college/middle/high school/student programs.

Outreach to the Homebound

- Staff can provide orientation sessions on how to operate the Oculus Go headset and then check it out to your homebound patrons who are able to comfortably use a headset on their own.
- For those requiring assistance to use the equipment, library staff can work with a caregiver or additional library staff person/volunteer to assist your homebound patron with their VR experience. You should never be alone in a space with a participant for your and the participant's personal safety.

Staff and Volunteers

The possibilities are limited only by your imagination when it comes to VR programs in and out of the library. Your staff and volunteers are key to your program's success. Identifying and recruiting staff and volunteers who are comfortable learning and using VR equipment, are willing to assist participants with the technology, show the ability to think and troubleshoot on the fly, *and* feel comfortable being in close physical contact with people will help you create a wildly successful program.

You can further increase staff and management support by encouraging them to try out the equipment themselves. This approach can also provide an opportunity for training and for your VR staff to build experience while working with participants they already know.

The optimal staff to participant ratio is one to one, especially for first-time participants. You can recruit tech-savvy volunteers to help decrease staff costs. As you and your staff become more experienced, this ratio may be able to be adjusted, especially if you stagger start times for other participants.

Safety

There are several safety considerations to keep in mind.

- Obtain a signed release for all participants aged eighteen and older and one with both a parent and teen signature for those aged thirteen to seventeen. Based on the current recommendations listed by Oculus, the use of VR equipment is not recommended for those under thirteen. NOLS also provides a copy of the health and safety information from Oculus, and the release participants sign has been approved by our insurance company/risk management and the library director.
- Offer a wheeled chair and/or keep one close by for participants who are standing.
- Vertigo, while rare, was the most common issue our participants experienced. Ask beforehand if your participants normally have issues with balance or vertigo. If any do, depending on the severity of their symptoms, tailor the suggested application based on their response. It is always a good idea to provide a chair to someone who does experience vertigo or balance issues.
- Ask participants if they are sensitive to heights. The "elevation" VR users experience during certain applications can feel very real, and some applications (Everest VR, for example) can be particularly intense. Again, tailor suggested applications to each participant and keep a chair on hand.
- Tape the floor. This can go a long way as a visual reminder for all observers, volunteers, and staff to stay clear of the VR participant since the person can't see you.
- Pay attention to where you are in the play space. When supporting participants, they can move suddenly, and you can (and probably will) get hit if you aren't mindful of where you are in relation to your participant.

- Pay attention to your participant's body language, movements, and commentary. Ask how they are doing—whether they are quiet or talkative—to communicate the fact that you are there. Ask them to let you know if they are having any discomfort and remind them that you can end the experience at any time.
- Remind participants that the fastest way to end the experience is to close their eyes, state that they are done, and remove the headset.

NECESSARY EQUIPMENT AND MATERIALS

- Four Oculus Quests
- Two Oculus Gos for outreach to the homebound and in-library checkout
- Application software from Oculus—there are many free apps to choose from, though paid apps can range from just a few dollars to up to $30 each. One account can include multiple headsets, which can share the apps to lower your cost.
- Access to a computer, laptop, tablet, or smartphone for setup and care of devices
- A laptop computer or television display that can be connected via Bluetooth to support your participants with physical and/or cognitive disabilities requiring assistance in accessing their VR experience
- Wheeled desk chairs without arms for a 360 experience for your participants who need or prefer to sit
- A surge protector for recharging devices when not in use (it is a good idea to keep the headsets on chargers when they are not being used)
- Blue painter's tape for marking the players' play space
- Chairs for observers
- Non-alcohol antibacterial wipes (Sani-Cloth) for cleaning headsets
- Silicon hygiene masks—at least two per headset to change between users and disinfect
- Disposable hygiene masks
- Microfiber cleaning cloth for lenses—do not use disinfecting wipes. A small amount of water can be used for stubborn smudges.
- Compressed air to blow out dust and other particles
- For cleaning and disinfecting equipment, *don't* use UV light as it can damage lenses.

Recommended but Optional Materials

- Oculus Quest Storage cases or a heavy-duty (Pelican-style) storage bin with or without a padlock. Some type of storage bin is recommended; library totes can work in a pinch.
- 360-degree camera(s) for creating your own content and/or for class-type instruction
- Battery packs for the headset to extend battery life. Consider using a VR Power battery; it offers a counterbalance for the headset and is designed to work with the Oculus Quest.
- Soft, low-profile, no-trip mats for participants to stand on
- Additional Oculus Gos for classroom-style and content creation programs

STEP-BY-STEP INSTRUCTIONS

Preparation

- Recruit the right staff and volunteers. Get yourself and your staff and volunteers comfortable with the use and care of the equipment and applications. You can't be expected to know everything about each application, though the more time you spend in the headset before putting it on someone else, the more comfortable you will be.
- Identify the best space to offer the VR experience. Meeting rooms, conference rooms, and, really, any open space in your library can work. Don't be afraid to set it up in the middle of your library outside on a sunny day—anywhere you have an 8 × 8-size space.
- Let your staff try it out on the clock. The best marketing for your library will be the excitement and enthusiasm your staff, managers, and even your library board have for the program.
- Don't let tech challenges get you down—they will happen. Everyone is there to have fun, and being able to laugh it off, think on your feet, and go with the flow will lead to a successful program.
- Set up the event's registration, if needed, using meeting room software or other methods used by your library. Space fifteen minutes between each participant for equipment cleaning.
- Check headsets for updates for firmware and applications prior to the session or on a regularly scheduled basis.
- Keep the headsets fully charged.

Program Instructions

- Set up the play space. Tape off an 8 × 8 area for each headset. Gather desk chairs. Each Go should always be used seated. The Quests can have participants seated or standing. Some applications recommend or require participants to do one or the other.
- Set up the equipment. A table can be used to hold the equipment when not in use, and headsets should be plugged in when not being used and between participants.
- When participants show up, go over the release form, then have them read and sign it before setting them up with the headset.
- Before having them put the headset on, show them the hand controllers and the headset and where the buttons are located. Explain that the controllers are universal and all applications can vary in what the buttons do since applications are created by different developers.
- Explain the application choices available to the patron before putting the headset on.
- Assist the participant with putting on the headset. When helping them put on the headset, explain what you are doing before you do it.
- For first-time users, provide a tutorial application in the headset to familiarize them with the controllers and what the VR experience is like.
- Launch the preferred application and assist the participant as needed throughout the experience.
- Ask participants to complete a short paper or digital program evaluation at the conclusion of the experience.

RECOMMENDED NEXT PROJECTS

There are many directions VR programs can go. Explore partnerships in the community to expand your program offerings. Purchase optional equipment, extra Oculus Gos, and 360 cameras to support classroom-style programs, during which participants can create their own content. Contract with a game designer educator to teach VR game design. The possibilities are many.

CHAPTER 2

Creating Dynamic, Immersive Field Trips with ClassVR and ThingLink

MELISSA ARENSON, Library Media Specialist
Pleasant Hill Intermediate School, Missouri

ClassVR is a stand-alone virtual reality (VR) headset designed for educational purposes only. Teachers and librarians can use the ClassVR educational platform to take users anywhere in the world, where they can experience different biomes and cultures and even outer space in a fully immersive, engaging manner! The ClassVR platform allows teachers and librarians to monitor all student activity while using the device; the platform also comes with the option for content to be delivered simultaneously to all users or for users to explore content at their own pace. ClassVR has partnered with ThingLink, giving teachers and librarians the ability to create deeper, more dynamic content. While the ClassVR platform does allow teachers and librarians to select premade content aligned with premade lessons, when used in conjunction with ThingLink, school and library staff can create virtual field trips that are fully immersive and can include sound, images, and web links all embedded within the VR content. Connections to curriculum are truly limitless with content created in ThingLink and uploaded into the ClassVR headsets!

Age Range	Type of Library Best Suited For	Cost Estimate
Kids (ages 3–7) Tweens (ages 8–12) Young adults (ages 13–18)	School libraries	$3,200–$5,000

PROGRAM CONSIDERATIONS

The content in ClassVR is adaptable to all age ranges. This project is adaptable for students both young and old. Older users will have more autonomy in exploring the accessed scene since they can manually navigate the controls on the side of the headset to access the content embedded into ThingLink. Younger students may struggle with using the controls. In cases of younger users, teachers can manually deliver the content to the device when they are ready, and all users can then view the same content concurrently. This prevents any distraction or frustration relating to control navigation for younger users while also preventing unsupervised exploration of the content.

ClassVR headsets come in sets of eight with a hard storage case that plugs into the wall. Each case includes a cooling fan that runs at all times, even when the sets are not in use. The case is fully padded on the top and bottom to protect the headsets and contains all the chargers pre-placed into each headset's storage location; so, there is no setup needed aside from plugging the case in. The case is designed to make transportation to classrooms easy and is similar to a small, rolling suitcase with a handle that can be stored inside the case when not in use. The cost of the headsets also includes a six-hour professional development session designed for up to twenty teachers. ClassVR flies a representative to your school at no extra cost to conduct this

FIGURE 2.1 When uploaded into ClassVR headsets, the interactive content icons flash for users who are in a fully immersive, 360-degree setting. Standard headphones can be plugged into the headset to further the immersive nature of the content and prevent distractions.

session, which covers all the basic functionality of the headsets and content platform. The professional development session can be customized to the school's specific needs in terms of in-depth content creation and delivery. This is only offered upon initial purchase. Any additional sets bought after the initial purchase will not include this session.

There is a mandatory annual $399 fee for ClassVR platform access, which is required to deliver the content to the headsets. This platform houses all curriculum created by ClassVR and all teacher/librarian-created content and is where content is loaded into the headsets for delivery to students. ClassVR will not function without this annual platform fee.

ThingLink offers several different levels of access, as follows: Free Teacher, Premium Teacher, and Schools and Districts. The Free Teacher option limits teachers/librarians to being the only content creators. There is no limitation to the amount of content a single teacher/librarian can create. However, there is a limited number of times the content can be viewed (one thousand times) annually on the free plan. A "view" in this sense occurs any time a user clicks on the interactive icons embedded in the content while in a VR headset. For example, if there are five interaction icons in your content, and you have ten students who each interact with all five icons, you have spent fifty views. Free plans are ideal for teachers starting out and wanting to practice. If using the plan with a full-sized class, however, the free views will run out quickly. The Premium Teacher plan allows teachers/librarians to create classroom groups and add students who can create their own content. This option is $35 annually and allows teachers/librarians to create classes of sixty students. For an increased cost, more students can be added via a customized plan. The Premium Teacher plan allows for twelve thousand views annually. School and District plans start at $1,000 per year. These plans allow unlimited classroom groups and students, unlimited content creation, and unlimited views, and are customized to the school district's needs.

A personal quote can be created upon contacting ThingLink. At any time, you can check how many views have been counted toward your account limit by viewing your account dashboard. Views are only applicable to content embedded as interactive icons in the content you've created. Feasibly, you could simply upload a 360 image with no embedded content, and it would not count against your total views regardless of how many times the content is loaded into ClassVR headsets because it is only a single image. "Views" only apply to the interactive icons you add to the 360-degree image.

OVERVIEW

ClassVR offers a full platform of educational content to be used with their headsets. This content includes videos, professionally created ThingLink content, and still images. Additionally, ClassVR now has an "explorable scene" content option, which allows users to walk around within the headset by manipulating the controls on the side of the headset. The majority of content on the ClassVR platform is limited to a single video or image, but more explorable scenes are being released regularly. Content on the ClassVR platform often comes with premade lesson plans, which makes these sessions literally a click-and-go lesson for patrons.

By using ThingLink to create your own content, you can develop multi-layered, immersive VR content that is then uploaded into the ClassVR headsets and is tailored to your needs.

Teachers and librarians can create a free or paid ThingLink account, create deep, dynamic content, and then upload it into the ClassVR teacher portal. That content can then be delivered to users via the ClassVR headsets. ThingLink content is fully customizable and limited only by the requirement of a 360-degree image. Any image taken from anywhere online or taken by the content creator with a 360-degree camera can be used as the basis for a ThingLink project.

Once a 360 image has been uploaded into ThingLink, teachers/librarians can then add interactive points of interest. These points can be text-only, text and an image, image only, or audio. There is no limit to the amount of interactive content that can be added to a single 360-degree image. When creating the content, interactive icons can be made to flash to draw users' attention to them, or they can simply be stationary icons users have to find before interacting. Background music can be incorporated to create a more immersive experience, or narration can be added by the creator to direct the user to the appropriate content and deliver any information desired while users explore the environment inside the headset. Because users are fully immersed in the content, any number of participants can access the content simultaneously.

NECESSARY EQUIPMENT AND MATERIALS

- An active ClassVR portal membership

- ClassVR headsets (one per participant or fewer—participants can take turns viewing the content)
- A free or paid ThingLink account

Recommended but Optional Materials

- Headphones or earbuds for each user
- An SD or USB storage device to expand the amount of content you can run on the ClassVR headset

STEP-BY-STEP INSTRUCTIONS
Preparation

- Charge ClassVR headsets fully.
- Create a ThingLink account (either paid or free depending on your needs). Since ClassVR offers a fully developed platform with premade lessons and content, a Free Teacher account is a great way to start practicing without paying until you are ready to push content out to the headsets for use by others.
- Find and download a 360-degree image. ThingLink offers 360 images on their site. You can also use Flickr; simply search on the Flickr website for a "360 image." Or you can download images from Google Street View, take your own 360-degree images with a specialized camera or via an app on your phone, search for images on Dreamstime.com or photopin .com, or just search Google for 360 images based on an applicable keyword or phrase. Truly, the options for finding 360-degree images ideal for your patrons are limitless as ThingLink has only a two-to-one size requirement ratio.

Program Instructions
How to Create Content in ThingLink

- Log in to ThingLink and click the blue *create* button at the top of the dashboard.
- Click *Upload 360/VR image.*

- Upload your image.
- Click *Add tag* from the left-hand menu.
- Select what you would like to add. Below are the various options available:
  - *Add text and media* allows you to upload an image as well as type in anything you would like users to learn about that image.
  - *Add text label* is an option that is limited to one hundred characters and is meant to be a quick label for an aspect in a larger image.
  - *Add content from website* allows you to add in video and audio files as well as anything created in the Google suite (Docs, Forms, etc.). For audio files, the embed code needs to be copy/pasted into your ThingLink creation. You can also upload images and videos directly from your device. Any site that offers an embed code can be embedded into your ThingLink creation. However, while ThingLink does allow you to add in videos and Google suite content, this content will not work in a ClassVR headset. It can be viewed via a computer for a less immersive experience, but ClassVR does not support third-party platform content outside of ThingLink.
- Add as many interactive icons as you like! Bear in mind that each student who interacts with each icon will count toward your total account views (see the costs listed in the section).
- As you add tags, you can select *change icon* to suit your needs. You can number your icons so users view them in a certain order. You can also select icons that will indicate whether they are images or audio or even upload images to be used as icons.
- When you have added all your interactive content, you can adjust the overall settings of the ThingLink project. Here, you can adjust icon colors, make interactive icons flash so users can more easily find them, remove ThingLink branding from the final product, and upload audio. Audio uploaded in the overall settings will continuously run as soon as the ThingLink content is opened. This audio can include ambient sound effects, music, or even a voice lecture that will pause when users interact with the icons. Background audio does not interfere with any audio from the interactive points of interest you create.

How to Upload Content into ClassVR

- Log in to your ClassVR portal and pen your ThingLink account dashboard.

- Click the three dots at the bottom-right side of the project you want to load into ClassVR.
- Select *Publish*, *Share Link*, and then *Copy Link*.
- Go back to your ClassVR portal.
- Select *ThingLink* from the bottom-right side menu.
- Paste the link into the search bar at the top of the ClassVR dashboard. You will see your content appear as lessons you can now deliver to users via the ClassVR headsets.

Note: You can follow the above steps to copy content from ThingLink that is premade for VR as well.

How to Deliver ClassVR Content to the Headsets

- Drag the content to the left-hand playlist bar.
- Either download or send the ThingLink content to the headsets at the bottom of the left-side menu.
    - If you plan to download the content, be forewarned that this course of action will take quite a while. So, it is best to do it the day before. Depending on the size and number of ThingLink(s) downloaded, it may take more than an hour. Downloaded content will go straight to the headsets and be stored on the internal memory, which can be expanded by an SD or USB storage device. Once downloaded, the content will play even if internet access is unavailable at that time.
    - Content can then be sent to the device relatively quickly, depending on the speed and reliability of your internet connection, though it will not work if the internet goes down or is too slow.

RECOMMENDED NEXT PROJECTS

If your students enjoy this method of learning about new places, the following sections of this book offer similar, alternative projects you can use to keep them engaged:

- Chapter 20: "Designing in Virtual Reality: Using Apps to Create and Make"
- Chapter 22: "Google's Tour Creator: Bringing Library and Classroom Tours to Life"
- Chapter 23: "Creating Immersive VR Library Tours with CoSpaces Edu"

Sculpting in VR
Using Oculus Rift + Medium

STEPHEN BARLOW, Technology Librarian
Mandel Public Library of West Palm Beach, Florida

P atrons can get in touch with their artistic side without all the mess by creating and manipulating virtual clay to create anything they can imagine with Oculus Medium! This program is great for introducing patrons to virtual reality, but it is flexible enough that physical and digital artists can pick it up and start creating masterpieces within minutes. Once their sculpting efforts are finished, they can easily be exported for 3D printing, video game creation, or other internet applications.

Age Range	Type of Library Best Suited For	Cost Estimate
Young adults (ages 13–18) Adults	Public libraries School libraries Academic libraries	$399–$3,000

PROGRAM CONSIDERATIONS

This program can be used by all ages, but the Oculus Rift safety guidelines state that it should only be used by ages thirteen and up.

The cost ranges from as low as $399 for only the Oculus Rift S headset to as high as $3,000 if you intend to purchase a high-end computer or laptop to

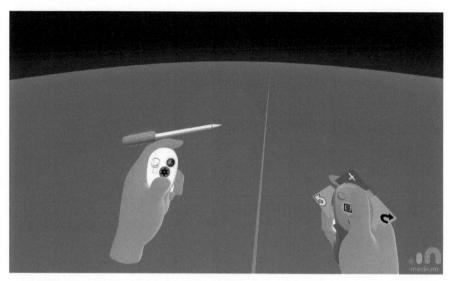

FIGURE 3.1   Main user interface for Oculus Medium

support your Oculus Rift applications as well. For the latter option, RAM is the most important factor. The Rift S headset works fine with 16 gigabytes, but 32 is recommended. Multiply this if you are buying more than one headset.

OVERVIEW

This application can be adapted for use in many projects but works well as an introductory class on how to use VR and adapt it creatively. A class of no more than *five is recommended* so that everyone has a chance to try it out. Time can be adjusted depending on class size and hands-on participation, but *between one and two hours is best per session*. One person is fine to lead this class, but if more than one headset will be used, it can be helpful to have an extra person for support during the hands-on portion. To add an extra dimension to the project, show how to export a file and print it out using a 3D printer.

NECESSARY EQUIPMENT AND MATERIALS

- At least one Oculus Rift S VR headset

- VR-ready computer
- Oculus Medium program
- TV or projector with video input connection (example: HDMI)
- Video export accessories (example: HDMI cable, adapter dongle)

Recommended but Optional Materials

- 3D Printer

STEP-BY-STEP INSTRUCTIONS

Preparation

- Familiarize yourself with the basic controls of the Oculus Medium software and how the sculpt tools work. Check out Oculus Medium on YouTube for a great list of tutorials.
- Develop a simple model that you want to create for your students that they can easily and quickly recreate. Be sure to create something that uses a couple of different stamps and requires one or two sculpting tools for editing. A snowman and tree are good examples.
- Clear an area in your classroom space that is large enough to allow for wide arm movements. If you have more than one headset, prepare accordingly.
- Set up and calibrate the Oculus Rift S headset(s) to make sure that movement tracking is working properly and batteries are healthy.
- Connect your computer to a TV or projector so that the participants can see what is going on in real time. Make sure that your display settings are set to mirror what is shown on the TV or projector.

Engage

- Begin the class by asking if anyone has ever used VR before, and if so, what kind of experience they had.
- Pass around the Touch controllers to show the proper way to hold them and the button placement on them.
- Explain how the headset works, where the cameras are, and how they work to track movement.
- Show the proper way to put on the headset and then enter the program.

Explore

- Use the TV or projector to show participants the mechanics of the program.
  - Show how the controllers are displayed in VR and what the buttons do.
  - Show how to change the dominant hand from right to left.
  - Add a few shapes and then show how the sculpt tools work.
- Now it is time to create a simple sculpt slowly while explaining what you are doing.
- When you are finished, show everyone how to export your 3D sculpt and what the file types can be used for.

Empower

- Have the participants choose who would like to go first and give them advice as they create their version of the model. If time allows, let them make their creation. Usually, ten to fifteen minutes is a good amount of time per participant.
- If you have some "free use" time for the VR headsets or want to create a series of classes, encourage participants to sketch out something that they want to create and have them work on it at the next session.

Bonus

- If you have a 3D printer available, you can also show how to export and print a small version of your sculpt while the other students are in the hands-on section of the class.
- Give participants access to the 3D printer at a later date to print out their models or offer to print them out for users at a later date.

RECOMMENDED NEXT PROJECTS

Depending on the programming you have at your library, you may be able to integrate this into other, larger projects. For example, if you have 3D printing classes, you can use VR applications to make creative chess or game board pieces. If you have video game creation programming, this is an excellent application for helping create character models.

Leveraging VR Software to Create Virtual Art Exhibitions

CAL MURGU, Digital Humanities Librarian

New College of Florida

n this chapter, you will learn the basics of how to create virtual exhibits for artwork using free (Artsteps) and licensed (art.spaces or Exhibbit) software. Creating virtual versions of art exhibits is a great way of extending the life of an art exhibit beyond its physical manifestation. Virtual exhibits can also be shared beyond your immediate community, letting many more experience your students' or patrons' artwork. Virtual reproductions of physical art exhibits are also an important option in the context of a pandemic where social distancing is required. Finally, these exhibits are virtual reality–enabled, meaning audiences will be able to explore exhibits using as little as a VR headset and mobile phone.

Age Range	Type of Library Best Suited For	Cost Estimate
Tweens (8–12) Teens (13–18) Adults	Public libraries Academic libraries	$0–$70

PROGRAM CONSIDERATIONS

Several options are available depending on your budget. This initiative can be completed entirely for free (assuming your library already owns a decent camera, scanner, or recent mobile phone). Virtual exhibits can be created at no cost using Artsteps; however, the overall quality will be more impressive if you choose to license specific software such as art.spaces or Exhibbit.

OVERVIEW

In this chapter, you will learn about some options available to you for creating VR-enabled online exhibits of artwork. While art exhibits are traditionally held in-person at art galleries for a specific period of time, certain circumstances, such as the COVID-19 pandemic, necessitate unique programming that enables us to continue to celebrate and share the work of artists. Virtual exhibit software enables us to recreate elements of an art show, including the experience of walking through and interacting with the artist and other attendees using VR gear.

For this project, you will be interacting directly with the artist and serving as the coordinator of the virtual exhibit.

NECESSARY EQUIPMENT AND MATERIALS

- A web-enabled computer
- A scanner, DSLR, or mobile phone with a decent camera
- VR headsets (can include low-budget gear, such as Google Cardboard, or a more high-performance option, such as HTV Vive)

STEP-BY-STEP INSTRUCTIONS
Preparation

- In academic settings, you can discuss the virtual exhibit with a studio instructor; in public library settings, discuss the virtual exhibit with your participants and their guardians.
- Consider the number of artists that will contribute artwork to your virtual exhibit. Depending on the software you choose and the number of participants/art pieces involved, you may need to increase your software licensing budget.
- Once you have established interest in your program, and depending on your budget, consider which software you would like to use for your

virtual exhibits. For a free option, choose Artsteps.com; for a licensed option, choose artspaces.kunstmatrix.com or exhibbit.com.
- Spend some time getting to know the functionality of each software by reading tutorials and reviewing official walkthroughs available online.

Program Instructions

Build Your VR Space

You can choose a default space for your virtual exhibit or create your own. Each software provides you with an option to create a unique virtual space that will house your virtual exhibit. You can place walls and select different colors and textures to create a unique space for your exhibit. Based on the number of artworks that you will display, roughly plan out how to distribute the art evenly throughout your exhibit.

Digitize and Upload Artwork

For best results, you and your participants should aim to digitize art at the highest resolution possible and save the image at its maximum quality. If possible, use a DSLR camera for this task. If you do not have a high-quality DSLR, you can use your cellphone camera in a well-lit environment.

For easy organization, create folders on your computer for each artist and include the following files in each: a high-resolution copy of the art as a JPEG or PNG file, the title and physical description of artwork in a text document, and an artist statement in another text document.

Upload the artwork and enter the appropriate metadata, such as the title, dimensions, physical description (medium), and artist statement. Then, "hang" the artwork in your virtual exhibit. Placement is important— remember that audiences will "walk through" your exhibit, so make sure to place the artwork at their approximate eye level.

Edit and Publish Your Exhibit

Create a description for your exhibit, including the participant names, and make your exhibit public by publishing it on the web.

Share and Embed Your Exhibit

Share a link to your exhibit with your participants and share it with your community over social media or other appropriate channels.

Consider embedding the exhibit on a dedicated page on your library website.

VR Station

Establish a space in your physical library where your community can experience the virtual exhibit using VR hardware. This can be done using relatively cheap products, such as Google Cardboard, or more elaborate options, such as an HTC Vive. Simply point your browser to the public URL of your virtual exhibit.

RECOMMENDED NEXT PROJECTS

For academic settings, consider offering this service as one of several digital scholarship opportunities for art faculty and students. For public library settings, this is a great programming opportunity to introduce patrons to community art programs and offers a low barrier of entry into VR.

If you enjoyed this programming idea, you may want to consider Chapter 15: "Virtual Reality as a Medium for Community Art," Chapter 21: "How to Create a VR Art Exhibition," and Chapter 25: "ArtEdge: A Multidisciplinary Art and Tech VR Experience for School Children."

Building a Community for Patrons in AltSpaceVR

PLAMEN MILTENOFF, Information Specialist
St. Cloud State University, Minnesota

n this project, faculty and/or staff from a public or academic library will transition their library services to patrons from the traditional face-to-face hybrid and/or online approaches to a virtual world (AltSpaceVR or ASVR). This project will provide librarians with a wide range of communication avenues with patrons as well as give them the opportunity to gamify certain processes and services and to prepare the library to deliver simulations, incorporate artificial intelligence through the Internet of Things, and incorporate data analytics. This use of virtual worlds will help the library and the campus to increase individualized learning.

Age Range	Type of Library Best Suited For	Cost Estimate
Young adults (ages 13–18) Adults	School libraries Academic libraries	$1,000–$1,500

OVERVIEW

In this project, librarians will "meet" their patrons—college and/or high school students—in a "playground" that is becoming increasingly popular—virtual worlds. The goal is to meet patrons in their "natural habitat"—gaming platforms, simulations, and other virtual world-type arenas. All the current types of assistance provided by libraries and librarians—live chat sessions; phone calls; and e-conferencing sessions, including audio and video—are all available communication tools offered in virtual software, with the addition of one very important element: the avatar. While patrons can choose and modify the appearance of their avatars, they also enjoy the ability to "see" their librarians' or peers' avatars (and their choices), thus personalizing the experience. Virtual worlds also provide librarians with important facilitator features not feasible in the real world. While the facilitator organizes students into groups who can wander and explore the world on their own, the facilitator also has the ability to "call on" session participants all around the world. Virtual worlds provide opportunities for cost-effective presentations, exhibitions, and simulations. Virtual worlds also provide opportunities to build/illustrate ideas, hypotheses, and final products in ways that would be costly, time-consuming, and ecologically unfriendly in the real world.

NECESSARY EQUIPMENT AND MATERIALS

- One to two Oculus Quest, Oculus Go, HTC Vive Focus, or Samsung Gear VR headsets
- AltSpaceVR (ASVR) social platform (to download on the headset)
- AltSpaceVR 2D mode (to download on each computer—Windows OS only)

Recommended but Optional Materials

- SideQuest app if you are using an Oculus headset

STEP-BY-STEP INSTRUCTIONS

Preparation

Novices not familiar with virtual worlds (e.g., Second Life, a popular app during the beginning of the century; Minecraft, popular during the early teens of the century; and/or almost any multiplayer virtual game) should familiarize themselves with the basics of movement and communication via the provided toolset beforehand. Training and experience are crucial in order to be able to move and converse freely in any virtual world whether that world is accessed via a keyboard and mouse on 2D mode on a Windows computer or via a virtual reality headset. The tools available for the presentation and facilitation of meetings and learning sessions require training and time to become comfortable within a VR environment, much like similar tasks in a face-to-face environment.

- Create two accounts/avatars in ASVR:
  – One for the VR headset
  – One for the 2D mode on Windows computers
- Practice controlling both avatars in the same ASVR world to become familiar with the advantages and disadvantages of each mode.
- Designate a meeting room for future activities either by adopting an existing one or building a new one within the system.
- Learn the different levels of accessibility and then assess, according to the goals of the future activities, whether each meeting room should be accessible to patrons of the library only or if they should be open to outside guests as well. As is the case with other social media platforms, each virtual world is equipped with different levels of privacy.
- Prior to hosting a virtual-world event, make sure all presentation tools are working and available to participants.
- The most effective presentations are conducted by a team: A wing person controls the 2D mode avatar, starts/stops the recordings, handles other logistics, and troubleshoots on-the-fly issues while the attention of the primary facilitator remains undividedly focused on the event's content and interaction with the patrons.
- Introducing novices to virtual worlds and VR can be challenging, especially if the patrons are not in the same physical space as the facilitator(s).
  – In the case of an online introductory session to the library virtual world environment, one way to organize the session is by using a synchronous approach: employ a familiar e-conferencing room (e.g., Zoom, Microsoft Teams, Google Meet, Facebook Messenger, WhatsApp, WeChat, etc.) and then guide your patrons through the initial steps in ASVR using the chat/audio/video/desktop-sharing capabilities of the e-conferencing room.
  – Another approach—an asynchronous one—can mimic the flipped classroom model, which prepares patrons with the intro and basics

of the virtual world by having them follow directions at home prior to the virtual-world session.

- Both synchronous and asynchronous approaches benefit greatly from peer support: Avoid a "lecturing" model; have patrons collaborate and communicate among themselves through the initial steps.

Program Instructions

For a Library Orientation Session

- Ask patrons to introduce themselves.
- Ask patrons to form teams or have the facilitator assign patrons to groups.
- If you have ASVR built into your library environment, split patrons into groups and have them engage in a scavenger hunt, earning rewards for each item/concept discovered.

For a Library Instruction Session

- Ask students to introduce themselves and group them according to similar majors/interests, etc.
- After demonstrating how to research, have students do research on their own and discuss their experience in groups. Co-facilitators can accompany groups and help when necessary and/or respond to questions/ inquiries.

For Library Events

- Meet and greet patrons and introduce the event.
- Discuss the event and let patrons participate in the discussion.
- Have appropriate interactive activity(s).

Explore

For each type of library engagement, co-facilitators can individually come up with engagement activities based on their familiarity and comfort with ASVR and with virtual worlds and multiplayer games in general. During the early stages of facilitating events in ASVR, similar to activities in a face-to-face environment, you should plan something relatively basic. For example, you can prepare a scavenger hunt for artifacts and trivia around a virtual world and encourage patrons to explore that world individually and/or in groups and then discuss their findings and experience. Advanced users of ASVR can prepare simulations and more interactive quests, which can include a scoring system with leaderboards and similar gamification amenities (e.g., Kahoot! can be easily incorporated into an ASVR session).

Empower

Allowing patrons to explore and build their knowledge boosts their confidence in using library services and conducting research on their own.

Patrons exposed to knowledge building in the library ASVR environment will be more receptive to other such knowledge-building environments in their fields of study, thereby increasing their comfort level with learning and using these tools.

If patrons are also faculty members, exposure to virtual learning will help them develop the skills and experience needed to incorporate interactive teaching and simulations in their courses.

Below are some sample questions to ask learners if an assessment system and/or leaderboard is in place (e.g., Kahoot!):

- How would you rate your group's experience throughout the scavenger hunt?
- What did you learn about research? How do you intend to conduct research in your topic/field based on the simulation/game you participated in during this session?
- How might you adapt your virtual world to accommodate better research methods?

Learning Outcomes

Participants will:

- Learn about library services and how to use them
- Describe library services and use them successfully
- Perform basic research in a multiplayer game environment and describe the importance of collaboration in research and of making connections across disciplines

- List some advantages of working in a virtual environment and describe how to prepare for similar environments in their fields of study and work

RECOMMENDED NEXT PROJECTS

If using ASVR with patrons is to your liking, the possibilities for developing new ways to engage users in this environment are virtually limitless. ASVR kits, which can be used to build your own worlds, are available for free, as is support for these kits. Numerous volunteers lead orientation sessions 24/7; share advice, objects, and codes you can use to develop and customize your world settings; and are happy to assist you in developing new engagement tools and learning simulations.

zSpace Open Lab
Using AR/VR Software to Learn Anatomy and More

CARI DIDION, Science Librarian

ELIZABETH STERNER, Health and Human Services Librarian

Governors State University, Illinois

I n this project, participants will navigate the zSpace augmented reality and virtual reality platform to engage in a variety of activities. Working with a laptop stylus and tracking eyewear, users can immerse themselves in an interactive, lifelike atmosphere. Participants will begin with activities designed to give them the skills needed to successfully manipulate objects in the VR platform using the stylus pen. Once they become savvy with the equipment, participants can explore a variety of software platforms. This open-lab platform allows participants to choose their own adventure.

Age Range	Type of Library Best Suited For	Cost Estimate
Tweens (ages 8–12) Young adults (ages 13–18) Adults	Public libraries School libraries Academic libraries	$10,000–$22,000

COST CONSIDERATIONS

Each laptop is roughly $1,800. Additional costs depend on software program add-ons, follower eyewear, computer mice, extension cords, etc. Alcohol-based cleaning wipes should be available for participants to wipe down the equipment and eyewear after use. Participants can work in groups of three using one laptop with follower eyewear.

OVERVIEW

A zSpace laptop and software components can be used to connect state curriculum standards to AR/VR experiences librarians can use to support standards-based learning. The subject areas explored in this program support STEM activities and include science (earth, space, life, physical), arts, math, social science, and engineering design. With a class set of ten zSpace laptops, up to thirty individuals may participate in one program session. To ensure adequate hands-on assistance and help with technical issues, this program should be run by two or more librarians/staff members. As can happen with any activity that relies heavily on the use of a visual screen, your users may experience VR-related headaches and or nausea. Scheduling frequent breaks is recommended throughout the one-hour session.

This program is designed to acclimate the first-time user with zSpace and is divided into two parts. The initial activity will help participants gain familiarity with the equipment by using the zSpace Demo package. This application highlights skills that will allow users to engage with a variety of activities and movements using the many attributes of the stylus tool. In this AR/VR setting, participants are seated at a table in a park. They can

FIGURE 6.1 Participants seated using a zSpace laptop to explore visible body human anatomy Atlas 8.0 software.

manipulate chess pieces on a chessboard or switch scenes by picking up one of six objects and dropping it into a glowing orb/portal. Scenes include a butterfly habitat, a robotic arm, a beating heart, a blueprint mock-up, a wristwatch dissection, and a playroom filled with toys. Ideally, each participant will explore all six scenes before moving to the open-lab portion of the program. In each scene, objects can be manipulated by turning or rotating the stylus and can be placed in a variety of positions or expanded to view up close. In the second half of the program, users will be allowed to access more advanced software such as zSpace Studio, Newton's Park, Franklin's Lab, zSpace Experiences, VIVED Science, Unity, Tinkercad, VIVED Chemistry, Labster, Human Anatomy Atlas, VIVED Anatomy, VR Canine Anatomy Training System by GTAFE, VR Automotive Mechanic, Wave NG, Leopoly, and many others. Participants can explore at their discretion as time allows.

zSpace can be used in online as well as blended learning environments. At our academic library, we created a flexible learning environment with the potential for users to check out the zSpace laptops for individual remote-learning opportunities. You can also record demonstrations of content that can be streamed or posted in your learning management system. If you have enough laptops available, you can use zSpace in a flipped classroom environment. Demonstrations can be recorded for review outside of the library, and laptops can be checked out for enriched virtual learning beyond the offerings of your institution; e.g., automotive mechanics.

NECESSARY EQUIPMENT AND MATERIALS

- A class set of ten zSpace laptops
- Ten sets of tracking eyewear glasses
- Ten stylus pens
- Twenty sets of extra follower eyewear glasses
- An internet connection
- Alcohol-based sanitizing wipes
- zSpace—available for purchase at https://zspace.com

Recommended but Optional Materials

- A screen and projector for demonstration
- One USB mouse (not necessary if your laptop has a touchpad)

STEP-BY-STEP INSTRUCTIONS

Preparation

- Familiarize yourself with the zSpace applications and various software packages.
- Sanitize all appropriate equipment.
- Set up and test the zSpace laptops before the session begins.

Program Instructions

- Ask participants to share any prior experience they have had using AR or VR. Talk about how the zSpace platform compares to their other virtual experiences.
- Break up participants into groups of three or fewer and assign them to a zSpace laptop.
- Discuss the anatomy of the zSpace laptop and identify the three sensors on it. Explain how the tracking system in the laptop interacts with the eyewear. Have them hold the stylus and discuss each of the three buttons and their purpose. Explain how the follower glasses allow participants to view the visual field and allow time for them to try on both sets of eyewear. Discuss proper positioning (patrons should keep both feet on the floor, maintain the correct posture, etc.).
- Instruct participants to open their Google Chrome browser and type in: go.zspace.com/content. Ask them to type in the search bar "zSpace Demo" and then click *Launch*.
- Ask participants to use the stylus to pick up a chess piece and set it down on another location on the board. Allow them to practice this skill.
- Explain how the glowing orb/portal allows users to access different scenes. Demonstrate by picking up the heart with the stylus and dropping it into the orb. Explore this scene by making the heart rate increase.
- Describe how the stylus buttons perform different functions in different environments.
- Allow participants to explore each of the six scenes.
- After the participants have completed all six scenes, ask them to discuss what they saw/felt. Did they like certain scenes better than others? Did they have greater success holding the stylus in a particular way? What

did they learn about the stylus buttons? This discussion naturally incorporates a rest break for weary eyes!

- Briefly discuss each of the following programs and their applications: zSpace Studio, Newton's Park, Franklin's Lab, zSpace Experiences, VIVED Science, Unity, Tinkercad, VIVED Chemistry, Labster, Human Anatomy Atlas, VIVED Anatomy, VR Canine Anatomy Training system by GTAFE, VR Automotive Mechanic, Wave NG, and Leopoly. Encourage participants to select three programs they would like to explore further and allow them time to interact with each one. Alternatively, you may assign groups to a program and have them report back to the larger group about their experience. Because this is likely their first experience with zSpace, they will be very engaged with the different programs. The open-lab concept offers participants the opportunity to explore the software in their own time and at their skill level. Remember to allow time at the conclusion of the session for a discussion as participants will likely be very excited about their experience.

- Ask participants to wipe down their equipment with an alcohol-based sanitizing wipe. Make sure that all the components are accounted for before dismissing the participants.

RECOMMENDED NEXT PROJECTS

The zSpace laptop has many applications, and the projects you can explore are virtually endless. For those interested in coding, the Tinkercad app, by Autodesk, gives users the ability to create 3D designs and then launch those designs in zSpace Studio. For an artistic crowd, Leopoly offers a digital sculpting mode in which users can choose from different design brushes and sculpt the sphere as if it were clay. The objects can be saved to files or printed using a 3D printer. For those interested in anatomy, Visible Body is equipped with quizzes and tutorials as well as the option to create slides that can also be saved to a file. Additional projects can be created for each of the software applications offered in the open-lab session.

360 Tours Made Easy, Scalable, and Useful

LIZ GABBITAS, **Technology and Innovation Coordinator**
Utah State Library Division

Virtual 360 tours provide a unique opportunity to bring people into your building in a new way. Using a virtual tour, you can share behind-the-scenes activity, open special collections to the public, or reintroduce the library to the community. Today's accessible 360 cameras and photo platforms make these virtual worlds easier than ever to create. Tours can be carefully curated experiences with professional photography and interactive elements or just be the product of a few hours of work by a teen with a smartphone. With some imagination, a virtual tour can be a library program, a tool for advocacy, and a springboard for creating lifelong library users.

Age Range	Type of Library Best Suited For	Cost Estimate
Young adults (ages 13–18) Adults	Public libraries School libraries Academic libraries	$0–$10,000

COST CONSIDERATIONS

Your intention for the finished product will determine the level of camera and platform needed. While most smartphones can take 360-degree photos

FIGURE 7.1 Clearly labeled hotspots help users easily navigate this library tour as they would in the physical space.

with a free app, such as Google Cardboard Camera, and publish to free platforms, the end result will be limited. To build 360 tours on a platform with a virtual reality mode and VR user interface, expect to spend $150 to $1,000 in annual subscription fees. A mid-range camera ($150 to $350) will produce high-quality photos for tours covering less than 50,000 square feet. For buildings over that size, costs may include such factors as hiring a professional photographer, renting a camera with laser sighting and distance measurements, and stitching together a complex tour with separately hosted pieces. Professional tour building services typically run from $0.10 to $0.20 per square foot, often taking total project costs over $10,000.

OVERVIEW

Virtual tours are easy to build and use accessible technology for quick impact. First, 360 photos capture the entire environment surrounding the camera rather than just what is directly in front of the lens. This is achieved by rotating the camera or with wide-eye lenses that capture a large field of view and then stitch the images together. Second, multiple images are displayed together with transition points between the images that mimic transitions in the real space such as following doors or hallways. Finally, the end viewer experiences a replica of moving in the real space. This virtual realism can go as far as immersive mixed reality (MR) by adding informational "hotspots"—interactive elements that display text, photos, sound, animations, or even videos.

Your virtual tour should be designed around the needs of your target audience. Is this tour meant to help English language learners feel comfortable visiting the library for the first time? Is it a tool to show legislators their hometown library, allowing them to see what has changed since their last visit and what has stayed the same? Is it meant to welcome young students to a new school? Your tour could also focus on your library's needs or goals. Perhaps your virtual tour will allow a teen advisory board to make a contribution to the library. Maybe you would like to design it as a way to encourage community input before a building remodel. No matter the purpose, the approach should focus on your unique needs.

NECESSARY EQUIPMENT AND MATERIALS

- 360-degree camera
- Virtual tour platform
- Laptop or desktop computer

Recommended but Optional Materials

- Tripod
- Phone, tablet, or Bluetooth remote for the camera
- Any VR headset or smartphone VR viewer

STEP-BY-STEP INSTRUCTIONS
Preparation

- Explore other virtual tours for ideas and inspiration.
    - Try looking at Matterport (matter port.com/industries/gallery) for general ideas, Google Arts & Culture (artsandculture.google.com/project/virtual-tours) for examples of museum tours, or Utah public libraries (kuula.co/profile/StateLibraryUtah) for specific program examples.

- Make a list of your goals with the finished tour.
  - What should be featured in your tour to meet your goals?
  - Where and how will your target audience access the tour? Possibilities include a browser, their own mobile devices, or a VR headset in the library.

- Make a plan for patron and staff privacy.
  - In the United States, public buildings are fair game for photographs; so, taking photos during regular hours of operation would likely not present any liability. However, courtesy suggests you alert patrons and staff of active photography sessions. Options include signs at entrances or throughout the building requesting that anyone entering the building sign a photo release or having the photographer wear a tag or sticker stating, "I'm taking photos."
  - Also not required by law but suggested by the ethics of librarianship is the removal of all personally identifiable information captured in the photo, including people's faces. Some platforms provide face blurring; others allow you to place images, such as a library logo or emojis, over faces and computer screens.

- Choose a platform that fits your specific needs.
  - What is your budget? Pricing for virtual tour platforms is often scaled; so, you may be able to get an otherwise expensive platform for less if you can forgo premium features.
  - How many scenes or rooms will be in your tour? How many tours will you have in total? Many platforms limit the amount of content you can upload or use based on your account or subscription level.
  - What type of navigation do users need? If you intend to show the tours in VR mode, you will need hotspots to move between scenes or rooms. "Look to select" or click-less hotspots will work with button-free VR headsets.
  - Do you need to embed text, videos, photos, sounds, or other special files?

Instructions

Photograph Your Library

- Sketch a map of the library and keep it with you while shooting. Draw an "X" wherever you take a photo and label the spot (e.g., "Stacks A Hall 2").
- Always shoot at the same height from the ground and never above six feet. Viewers will expect the picture to be near their own eye level or lower.
- Use a tripod and camera remote or app so the photographer is not in every shot.
- Consider whether retaking photos would be difficult (for instance, if you are renting the camera). If so, take multiple photos in each spot a few moments apart.
- Save the photos to your computer and name the files using your labels from the map (e.g., "stacksA2 001.jpg"). This will save you time while building.

Build Your Tour

- On your map, draw one path through the library that intersects each photo location. This step may require you to double back or retrace your steps.
- Upload your image files. Add them to the tour in the order they appear on your map. If you are planning a large tour, upload and build one area of the library at a time. Clear file names will help.
- Starting with the entrance, add a hotspot to take the viewer to the next photo. Place the icon near where the viewer would physically travel (e.g., in the hallway or at an elevator door). If moving between rooms, clearly indicate where the hotspot will take them. For instance, display an icon with the text "Go to Circulation."
- Continue adding hotspots until all the photos are connected.

Add Informational Hotspots, Highlights, or Interactive Elements

- Informational hotspots could include factoids about the building or collection; the schedule for regular programs at your library, such as story time; or even a book recommendation.

- Try embedding videos, such as preservationists at work, storytellers entertaining a crowd, or a staff member asking, "How can I help you?"

Publish Your Tour and Share It with the Community

- After publishing, make sure the tour is visible and navigable from different browsers, on mobile devices, etc. To test all this from a laptop or desktop, open the tour as a regular user. Type Ctrl + Shift + I (Chrome) or Command + Option + I (Safari) to open the *Inspect* function (or follow the menu options in Firefox or Microsoft Edge). Once the *Inspect* window is open, toggle between different types of devices and refresh to test operability.
- To share the tour on your library's website, embed it as a photo or video player. Most platforms provide the necessary HTML free of cost. Additionally, you could add one image from the tour as a slowly panning 360-degree banner image, which links to the full tour when clicked.
- Try advertising your tour on your library's social media platform. Facebook's photo upload tool looks for metadata identifying photos as 360-degree images and automatically displays them correctly. This is a great tool to generate interest and bring users to your website.

Tips & Tricks

- Do a short, quick, and easy test tour from beginning to end with two or three photos, simple transitions, and an informational hotspot. This will help you troubleshoot the process before spending time photographing the whole library.
- For a consistent sense of movement throughout a tour, try to make sure that each shot includes the floor where the tripod will go for the next photo. Use an icon of footprints at the center of the next tripod location for the hotspot that takes the user forward. Your viewers will easily understand the navigation and feel solidly oriented in the digital environment.
- If using no-click navigation, such as "look to select" hotspots, place your navigation hotspots above or below the horizon line. This will stop viewers from accidentally selecting the hotspot while just looking around.

- Low-budget VR goggles for smartphones are available in bulk for as little as $1 each. These make great giveaways and can be printed with a QR code or URL to direct people to the library's virtual tour.

RECOMMENDED NEXT PROJECTS

- Use a virtual tour of your library to introduce teens to the technology behind VR. After letting them try VR firsthand (See Chapter 1: "Virtual Reality Is for Everybody: Connecting with Harder-to-Serve Populations," and Chapter 10: "Integration and Application of Virtual Reality in Library Programming," for ideas), let them explore the library in the tour. Then ask them to express the difference between experiencing a digitally rendered environment and the videos or images from your tour. Additionally, you could ask them to identify components of the 360 tour. What technology was needed to create it? How do those components relate to the technology in the VR headset?
- Assign a teen advisory board or small group of students to create a 360 tour of the library or school. Approachable technology means teens can build their own virtual tours with minimal instruction, showcasing their unique view of the world and strengthening their confidence in the digital environment. When instructing teens on building tours, keep in mind various levels of comfort with different equipment. Some may prefer to use smartphones and skip the tripod while others may gravitate toward the best 360 camera you can provide. Allowing for flexibility with the process and outcome will encourage teens to take creative risks.
- Invite your patrons to participate in a community gallery of tours from all over town. Create a lending kit with a 360 camera and tripod. Include instructions for a free and easy online platform such as Google Poly. Encourage patrons to check out the kit and build their own tours. Patrons could feature their school, classroom, or office; local landmarks; favorite locations around town; and more. Debut the community gallery in coordination with a citywide event or festival.

How to Create Augmented Reality Culture Expedition Experiences

XIAOLIAN DENG, Senior Librarian of Reference and Technology

The County Library, Salt Lake County, Utah

Metaverse Studio is a visual programming tool for creating augmented reality experiences and interactive content. The tool is easy to use; you will not face a steep learning curve to master the skills you need. With Metaverse's drag-and-drop storyboard canvas, you can create interactive experiences by combining components such as scenes and blocks and placing them in the proper sequence. You can load your AR experiences to any IOS or Android device. Metaverse is an exciting and affordable technology to teach basic programming and AR.

Google Earth Projects are comprised of creation tools that allow you to create customized maps and stories about your world, along with any variety of places or cultures. You can save places and information and add text, photos, and videos all in one project to complete your collection within your map-based story. You can create projects based on topics of your choosing such as culture expeditions, historical landmarks, virtual tour trips, games, and scavenger hunts. These tools allow you to share your project and collaborate with others.

Google Expeditions, an immersive learning app, takes you on virtual reality field trips to explore amazing places such as the new Seven Wonders of the World.

CoSpaces Edu is a platform that allows you to make AR and VR creations with user-friendly tools. You can build and code your own experiences in

3D AR and VR environments anywhere from a tablet or smartphone; use a visual, block-based programming language to add interactions; and view your creations in VR or AR in real-time.

The Koji platform app allows you to remix and create interactive posts and games by customizing images, sounds, texts, and more. After you create your posts, you can share them on your social platforms or embed them on any website.

Throughout this project, you and your community can combine these amazing technologies or use them separately to create interactive culture expeditions, virtual field trips, interactive stories, AR camera frames, AR games and quizzes, scavenger hunts, breakouts, and countless other offerings that can extend learning and help your patrons experience the world in new ways. This project blends goals of strengthening digital literacy, creativity, and logical thinking with collaboration, engagement, imagination, goal-setting, and empowerment. You can create adult programs, such as virtual 360 armchair travel, to boost cultural awareness, as well as programs that appeal to younger groups, such as coding, creating/remixing apps, games, and breakouts, to extend learning in a fun way. These virtual expeditions can provide a virtual social gathering place with AR/VR social platforms for your community; develop teamwork as your patrons work and create together; help your community learn basic programming, coding, app remix and creation, and computer science fundamentals; and boost their observation and problem-solving skills while helping them master the fulfillment of creative ideas in a unique way. This project is suitable for different age groups and offers a wide coverage of various topics to choose from.

Culture Expeditions
@sanref
Explore sensory expeditions without leaving your home!

FIGURE 8.1 Culture Expeditions metaverse app QR code.

Age Range	Type of Library Best Suited For	Cost Estimate
Kids (ages 5–7) Tweens (ages 8–12) Young adults (ages 13–18) Adults	Public libraries School libraries	$0–$3,000

Costs will depend on the hardware and devices purchased. Cheap devices may cost as little as $35 each with universal VR Goggles or as high as $1,000 each with Apple iPad Pro (you are not required to purchase the high-end iPad with this software).

OVERVIEW

The main purpose of the culture expeditions AR program is to engage your community to enhance their digital literacy skills and build cultural and social understanding and empathy by creating together. This program can lead your community to create their own interactive experiences using communication, observation, and problem-solving skills and innovative thinking by adapting various technology tools and resources. Beginning-level participants in this project will learn how to create their own AR learning experiences using Metaverse Studio as well as learn how to arrange components, such as scenes and blocks on a storyboard canvas, and arrange them in the proper order. They will learn how to create customized maps and stories about a culture expedition tour of their choice using Google Earth Projects. They can use CoSpaces Edu's built-in tools and elements to create anything in 3D and let their imagination unfold. They can also have fun remixing and creating their interactive posts by using Koji mini-apps. You can also simply let Google Expeditions guide them through its virtual collections of 360 scenes and 3D objects to help them discover and explore destinations without having to leave their buildings. More advanced learners can build their own scene characters and 3D objects and models from scratch using Google Poly Tilt Brush and Blocks. They can create virtual stories by integrating texts and 360 photos and videos to present fantastic places around the world with Google Tour Builder or design themed virtual exhibitions, build immersive 360 tours, program games, and create interactive stories with CoSpaces Edu tools. One to two hours maximum is a sufficient block of session time for beginning-level projects. For more advanced-level projects, such as those involving coding and programming, the time allotted for each session may need to be extended. Ideally, each project should include four to five sessions/lessons. Consider recruiting student volunteers to assist with coding and computing projects. Smaller-sized classes totaling around ten to fifteen people are easier to manage for this type of program.

NECESSARY EQUIPMENT AND MATERIALS

- Android/IOS phones
- Desktop, laptop, tablets, iPads, or Chromebook
- Metaverse Studio and app
- Koji platform
- Google Earth desktop and app
- Google Expeditions app
- VR Goggles
- CoSpace Edu app
- The Google Tour Creator
- A 360 camera
- Google Poly Models
- A subscription to the CoSpaces Edu Pro plan

Recommended but Optional Materials

- One Oculus Rift headset
- Oculus Go
- Oculus Quest
- Smart TV
- Merge Cubes
- Subscription to ARKit yearly plan

STEP-BY-STEP INSTRUCTIONS

Preparation

- Make sure all the apps are downloaded and the devices are fully charged.
- Make sure participants have their Google accounts set up before the program starts for the beginner group program.

- Make sure participants have their personal accounts set up (in addition to their Google accounts) for the more advanced group program.
- Recruit expert volunteers for computer programming and coding if you do not feel comfortable educating others.
- Demonstrate your useful VR/AR resources.
- Choose the theme/topics of interest, such as national parks, historical landmarks, holiday traditions, famous people, literature sites, etc., respectively, according to the program group or level and so forth.
- Make sure all your tools or software are provided for your targeted participants' group accordingly.

Choose Your Software

- The Metaverse app works best with IOS devices for Google Earth presentations and the Google Art remix app.
- CoSpaces Edu offers a basic plan that is free with limited features. Their pro plan subscription fee is based on the number of seats purchased and includes all the available features such as code with all the CoBlocks or script languages, their built-in physics engine, a remix of CoSpaces from Gallery Go, and more.
- For Google Earth Projects, have a desktop, laptop, or Chromebook ready for each participant. Compatible web browsers include Chrome, Firefox, Opera, or Edge (Google Chrome 67, Firefox 63, Opera 54, or Edge 79). Make sure to set up a Google account that can be used with these devices and that the hardware acceleration is turned on. Be advised that you can view but cannot create projects on mobile devices.
- AR development toolkits, such as ARCore, ARKit, and Vuforia, are great for more advanced projects. ARCore supports both the IOS platform and Android, and it's free. ARKit supports only the IOS platform and requires a yearly subscription fee. Vuforia supports both IOS and Android; the free version has the Vuforia watermark, and the paid plan starts at $99 per month.

Engage

- Market programs via your social media platform or website and encourage participants to choose the thematic topics for your projects.
- Have participants choose places or countries they would like to see.

- Allow participants to create their own virtual tour of choices.
- Create decorations according to the countries or places chosen.
- Serve ethnic food or snacks based on the chosen countries or places.
- Play relevant music or include some trivia to enhance the projects.
- Demonstrate that your culture expedition's topics can be engaging and fun to learn.

Explore

- Allow some playtime for participants to get familiar with the basics of the platforms they will be exploring throughout the program.
- Guide your participants through their first AR experiences—particularly your beginning-level groups—and make them feel comfortable and supported.
- Ask your participants to write down any details they want to include about the countries or places in their virtual tour.
- Download or upload any photos and videos they want to use (remind them to only select images/videos labeled for noncommercial reuse with/without modification or to upload their own).
- Ask them what they feel were the highlighted aspects of the expedition? Discuss what the details of the expedition were.
- Encourage your participants to collaborate with peers to solve problems and challenges.
- Show their creations, receive and listen to feedback from others, and make improvements to their projects if necessary.
- Ask participants what tools they used to create these exhibitions and how they built their stories and make certain choices.

Empower

- Empower your participants to program and play their designed or remixed games in innovative ways using new technologies.
- Have your participants try to build 360 tours with different platforms, such as Google Earth, Google Tour builder, or CoSpaces Edu; get them to organize their research results; and then show and discuss the different experiences, points of interests, and knowledge gained by your users about the community, culture, or civilization during their creations.

- Ask your participants to use their imaginations to develop a story related to the project theme by combining their storytelling abilities with your available technology tools.
- Empower your participants to design a virtual exhibition on any topic of their choice.
    - Highlight the favorite parts of their creations.
    - Create descriptions or stories set in these places.
    - Show historical places and facts.
    - Visualize their projects in VR or AR mode and even project them onto the TV screen.

RECOMMENDED NEXT PROJECTS

There are many similar programs you can combine or create once your patrons have mastered this program, including:

- Combining your AR projects with other coding programs
- Creating an AR art exhibition with a 360 virtual tour of the artist and their artworks
- Creating apps with ARCore—targeted toward advanced learner groups

You may also explore the following programs in this book:

- Chapter 2: "Creating Dynamic, Immersive Field Trips with ClassVR and ThingLink"
- Chapter 3: "Sculpting in VR: Using Oculus Rift + Medium"
- Chapter 7: "360 Tours Made Easy, Scalable, and Useful"
- Chapter 23: "Creating Immersive VR Library Tours with CoSpaces Edu"

Exhibiting Digital Collections Via Web-Based 3D Galleries and Events

Using Mozilla Hubs and Other WebXR Frameworks

COLIN PATRICK KEENAN, University Library Specialist

North Carolina State University Libraries

n this project, you will build a custom online gallery space using Mozilla's free and open-source Hubs framework. WebXR technology allows us to utilize the internet's underlying strength: delivering the same web page to countless different web-browsing devices in the form best suited to each device. Utilizing this capacity, a user's smartphone, desktop computer, or even VR headset can choose the form of your gallery best suited for its capabilities without the need for you—the developer—to specifically build for more than one format or hardware configuration. WebXR technology is great for exhibiting media from library collections, highlighting solicited submissions, or hosting a meetup in a custom virtual space. It's also a great way to make VR content for which a headset is an *additive* rather than a requirement or barrier to entry.

Age Range	Type of Library Best Suited For	Cost Estimate
Tweens (ages 8–12) Young adults (ages 13–18) Adults	Public libraries Academic libraries	$0–$250

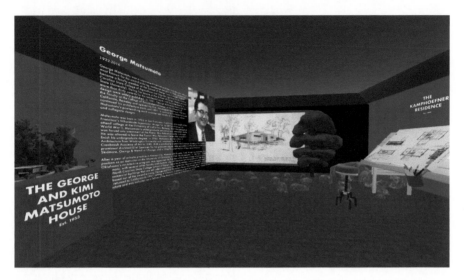

FIGURE 9.1   NC State University libraries have used online 3D galleries to highlight digital archives and special collections the public may not otherwise encounter. The "Modern Raleigh" exhibition highlights the career archives of such North Carolinian architects as George Matsumoto, as seen here.

COST CONSIDERATIONS

- All technologies described herein are currently available for free.
- Some institutions may prefer to utilize Hubs Cloud, an off-the-shelf AWS package, to host your Hubs content on your own dedicated server space (allowing greater customization of branding and security options) for less than $0.25/hour of server time.
- Excellent 3D-modeled gallery and venue templates are available on marketplaces such as Sketchfab and Turbosquid. These models can often be purchased for less than $10 and provide outstanding value and immediate polish.

OVERVIEW

Mixed Reality (MR) and Extended Reality (XR) experiences can be easily shared over the web via a technology framework called WebXR. This means that one can access virtual experiences, galleries, and events by simply clicking a link or navigating to a URL on the web.

The beauty of developing your library's own WebXR gallery is that you're in control of what it contains and how it is shared. You can make this as simple as a 3D web page that users browse at their own convenience with no social element. You could open it only at specific hours and have users meet one another there to interact or to "host" speakers. You can even make the gallery a functional "template" from which participants can spin off their own instances, letting them choose who they'll invite in via a link. By making your own WebXR Hub, you set the rules that best suit your library and its needs (without relying on a technology company to decide that for you). After all, who knows your library's needs better than you?

NECESSARY EQUIPMENT AND MATERIALS

- One desktop computer with the graphics processing capacity for 3D modeling and 3D development (sometimes referred to as a VR-ready computer)
- A reliably fast internet connection for that machine during development
- A VR headset *is not* required to build or experience anything described in this project.

Recommended but Optional Materials

- The more web-browsing devices (and internet-connection strengths) you test your prototype on, the stronger your overall gallery will be. Test on the devices you expect your visitors and participants to utilize (e.g., smartphones from past model generations)!

STEP-BY-STEP INSTRUCTIONS
Preparation

- Quality development and design begin by setting aside an appropriate amount of time. As the developer of this gallery, schedule yourself no less than three separate one-plus-hour blocks to engage with this project.
- Download Mozilla Firefox (or another browser that similarly supports the free and open internet).

- Take a moment to familiarize yourself with our compendium of resources for novice Hubs developers at https://go.ncsu.edu/hubskickstart. We'll make repeated mention of this compendium within this chapter since it is a living document that will be updated with the latest status of the tools and techniques described here. There are videos, documentation, and other resources that our libraries have found invaluable in developing our earliest WebXR spaces and events with Hubs.

Program Instructions

- Collect the media and collections you'll want to incorporate into your hub gallery.
    - Your library may house special collections and archives, or you may wish to utilize open-access collections such as those offered by the Smithsonian Institute or the Library of Congress.
    - If you choose to solicit community contributions, the key is to deliver clear directions on the types of submissions you will accept. Offer dimensions, resolution, file format, and other pertinent information regarding the media you want to accept and showcase. Consider sharing a template and examples of submissions.
- After your submissions or curations are all saved in one location, begin the process of preparing them for inclusion in an online space. This process of "web-optimizing" such media to reduce their loading times and improve the performance of the overall scene relies on small improvements to every asset in the scene.
    - Specific, current guidance is given in the linked compendium (including guidance on using Blender to compress images and textures to 1024 × 1024 px or below to greatly improve scene performance).
- It can be very helpful to store all your media submissions in a single folder, saving your compressed media to a new folder as they become ready for incorporation into your gallery. This technique seems redundant at first but can prevent a lot of headaches later in your process, especially if you're managing dozens of media items!
- Following the guidance in our compendium, use the browser-based Mozilla Spoke editor to construct your 3D scene. Working from a template or "remixing" an existing Hub is a great way to build familiarity with the editor, and we've provided a few remixable Hubs in our compendium.

There are also several linked hour-long videos designed to familiarize you with all aspects of Spoke while building your demo scenes.

- As your scenes become more complicated, you may prefer to do most of your editing inside the free, open-source 3D editor Blender. It's an excellent tool with a plug-in for direct export to Spoke. This is detailed in the compendium.

- Save your work frequently! Save it as a backup project occasionally as well. Web tools are accessible and convenient, but nothing is more discouraging than losing work because your internet went out or your browser encountered an issue.

- Once your scene starts to shape up, you're going to want to see the scene from a first-person perspective to make sure it's acting as you expect. Try not to go more than an hour at a time without pressing *Publish*. This process will take a bit of time since it is an upload—a great opportunity for a stretch break.

  - Upon publishing, you'll receive a great color-coded "report card" that summarizes the complexity of your scene and its performance against suggested benchmarks. Some of these are more important than others. For example, the number of "materials" in your scene is suggested to be less than 25, but our experience indicates that, so long as these images are compressed, a scene will not lag in performance until it's near one hundred individual textures. Mobile devices will see a performance drop-off long before desktop devices do; so, consider your intended audience in this evaluation.

- Repeat this process of developing, publishing, and testing. The more individual testing cycles you complete, the better the gallery will look.

- In your Hubs gallery, use the *Share* button at the top of the screen to acquire a short URL. While you're in the Hub, you can share this with other people so they can test the gallery. Testing with multiple users is a great way to find issues you've lost sight of. As developers, we often begin to overlook glaring issues when we work on a project for long enough.

- Once your gallery is ready, you can disseminate the work!

  - If you want visitors to be able to launch their own individual instances of the gallery, share the Scene URL (it will have the word "scene" in the URL) so they can select *Create a room with this scene*.

  - If you prefer to share a scene that visitors will occupy alongside one another, it is a good idea to (after creating a room from your scene) open *Preferences* under the main menu and check the box titled *Disable auto-exit when idle or backgrounded*. Now you can share the URL for this individual instance (maybe via a redirected shorthand link), and others will be able to join the same room.

- – I often disable the ability for visitors to "pin" items in Hubs rooms by opening *Room Settings*. This prevents visitors from making alterations to the gallery.

RECOMMENDED NEXT PROJECTS

You may choose to explore other similar projects included in this book such as:

- Chapter 4: "Leveraging VR Software to Create Virtual Art Exhibitions"
- Chapter 21: "How to Create a VR Art Exhibition"
- Chapter 24: "Creating VR Exhibits Based on Digital Collections"

Integration and Application of Virtual Reality in Library Programming

CHLOE HOVIND, Assistant Librarian

SHELBY CARROLL, Assistant Librarian

Indiana University–Bloomington

n this program, library patrons of all ages will have the opportunity to test out and explore virtual reality on the Oculus Quest and Oculus Rift S via a VR Exploration session. This program is designed to be an introductory encounter with VR in a safe and friendly environment to encourage participants to not only have an initial exploration into VR but also begin a conversation about the future and any concerns they may have regarding these advanced technologies. Furthermore, this VR Exploration program is designed as a fun method for libraries to introduce new technologies into their communities while increasing exposure and use/circulation of their materials. Through this program, participants will learn how to properly and safely operate Oculus hardware, think more broadly about VR implications and opportunities, and gain excitement about and familiarity with the scope of what libraries can offer. Simple applications are available for librarians and staff to guide users through the program depending on their interests and thoughts about VR. These sessions can be done as part of a larger library community outreach event or as an individual programming event.

Age Range	Type of Library Best Suited For	Cost Estimate
Tweens (ages 8–12) Young adults (ages 13–18) Adults *The Oculus age recommendation is for ages 13+	Public libraries Academic libraries	$399–$1,800

FIGURE 10.1 Authors Chloe and Shelby assisting students with Oculus VR headsets during the VR exploration workshop

COST CONSIDERATIONS

Depending on the hardware already available, some libraries may need to purchase desktop computers with, at minimum, an Intel i3-6100 processor. Our library purchased a Dell Inspiron with an i5 9400 processor at a cost of about $650 for our Oculus. Any supplemental Oculus machines wanted or needed for the program would be an additional $399 each and would require another computer (per Oculus machine) with the same capabilities. Furthermore, depending on which applications are chosen for use in your exploration sessions, you may need additional controllers or equipment (such as the Oculus Gamepad or additional sensors).

Applications can also vary widely in price, ranging from free to $39.99. Given the exploratory nature of our program, simple applications, tutorials, and tours are recommended as they are typically less intense and require less specific knowledge of game and technology mechanics. These types of applications generally tend to be less expensive than more moderate-to-advanced user applications such as role-playing or first-person shooter games.

OVERVIEW

This program, or VR Exploration session, has been used successfully in various settings at the Sciences Library at Indiana University Bloomington. Our VR Exploration program was done initially during IU's Science Fest, an annual community outreach event that helps inspire citizens of Bloomington and students at the city's university to explore the institution's available resources and advancing technologies. During the event, librarians and student library assistants guided participants in the exploration of Oculus Rift S and Oculus Quest technologies within the Sciences Library during twenty-minute sessions. Participants were given an introduction to the technology and equipment and then asked to complete two tutorial applications that taught the basics of manipulating the digital environment. Once they completed the tutorials, patrons were able to choose from a variety of applications to explore on their own.

This program can also be completed outside of a community outreach event. We explored this option through a regularly programmed library series called Maker Mondays, a weekly event hosted by IU's Mini Makerspace. This program was open just to IU affiliates (students, staff, etc.), to give regular patrons of the library an opportunity to learn about the university's educational resources.

In both settings, sign-up sheets were used to regulate the flow of participants, and questionnaires were completed to help gauge the prior knowledge of patrons as well as their overall experience with the program. Before, during, and after each patron's experience, the library assistants encouraged conversations about VR to help inspire learning and thoughtful engagement with the VR application that reached beyond entertainment.

NECESSARY EQUIPMENT AND MATERIALS

- Oculus Rift S and/or Oculus Quest, which includes a headset and two remote controllers
- Optional Oculus accessories such as the Gamepad and Sensor
- Masking/painter's/duct tape to designate floor play space areas
- Measuring tape for designating minimum play space requirements (optional)
- Sanitary wipes to clean controllers and headset(s) between users

- Ethernet cable
- Large, empty room or dedicated space that is equipped with an ethernet port and electrical outlets
- PC compatible with necessary requirements for the Oculus Rift S (see table below)
- Depending on the purposes of the program (outreach, educational, etc.), a questionnaire the librarian/participant can complete to gather feedback for future programs and collect data for administrators

Minimum PC Requirements for the Oculus Rift and Oculus Rift S*

COMPONENT	RECOMMENDED SPECS	MINIMUM SPECS
Processor	Intel i5-4590/AMD Ryzen 5 1500X or greater	Intel i3-6100/AMD Ryzen 3 1200, FX4350 or greater
Graphics Card	NVIDIA GTX 1060/AMD Radeon RX 480 or greater	NVIDIA GTX 1050 Ti/AMD Radeon RX 470 or greater
Alternative Graphics Card	NVIDIA GTX 970/AMD Radeon R9 290 or greater	NVIDIA GTX 960 4GB/AMD Radeon R9 290 or greater
Memory	8GB + RAM	8GB + RAM
Operating System	Windows 10	Windows 10
USB Ports	1x USB 3.0 ports	1x USB 3.0 port
Video Output	Compatible DisplayPort video output	Compatible miniDisplayPort video output (miniDisplayPort to DisplayPort adapter included with Rift S)

*This table can be found directly on the Oculus website at https://support.oculus.com/248749509016567/?locale=en_US.

STEP-BY-STEP INSTRUCTIONS

Preparation

- Download the necessary software. The software can be found at https://www.oculus.com/setup.

- Set up the Oculus technology according to the step-by-step directions.
  - You can find directions for setting up the Oculus Rift S at https://support.oculus.com/1225089714318112.
  - You can find directions for setting up the Oculus Rift at https://support.oculus.com/857827607684748.
  - You can find directions for setting up the Oculus Quest at https://support.oculus.com/855551644803876.
- Download the apps that you wish to use during the program. Applications can range from $2.99 to $39.99. There are also many free applications available. The authors of this chapter used the following free applications: Oculus First Steps, Oculus First Contact, Google Earth VR, Catch a Mimic, and Disney Movies VR.
- It's best to have a sign-up system in place ahead of time to ensure all interested participants have enough time to have a memorable interaction with the technology. Use twenty- to thirty-minute time slots to allow participants to complete the initial tutorial as well as try out an additional application(s).
- Be sure that library staff and assistants are familiar with the technology, controls, and applications that they wish for the patrons to experience to offer direct support and troubleshoot any issues if necessary.

Session Setup

- Set up the desktop computer in the area where the program will take place. It is best to put the desktop on a small table or desk that can be placed at the perimeter of the area near an ethernet outlet.
- Clear the space of any additional chairs or tables.
- On the floor, take the tape and draw out a large square (we recommend at least 6 × 6 feet). This will be the designated play space for patrons.
- Turn on the computer and open the Oculus software.
- You will need to define the play space using the Oculus Guardian before your session begins to ensure the play space is within the lines of the tape. This will also give you a chance to ensure all your equipment is working properly.
- Use sanitary wipes to clean headset and controllers between users.

Program Instructions

- Welcome your participants! It's helpful to ask them about their previous VR experience (if any) right off the bat to guide which applications you encourage them to try.
- Assist the participant in placing the headset and controllers in the right positions.
- From the desktop computer, use the mouse to select *Oculus First Steps* to start the initial tutorial. This will automatically lead into *Oculus First Contact*, which is the second tutorial.
  - These tutorials are beneficial because it will give you (the librarian) a chance to get a feel for how comfortable the participant is and what kind of application they will want to try next (experiential vs. interactive).
  - Participants can easily spend their whole twenty-minute session in just the tutorial as they explore all the different interactions.
- From there, you can coach/suggest to your participant which application they might wish to try next:
  - If they are new to VR, you might suggest an experiential app, such as Disney Movies VR, or any virtual tours.
  - If they are newer to VR but are quickly gaining familiarity with it, you might suggest more interactive applications, such as Google Earth VR or Catch a Mimic, or another app with basic controls.
  - If the participant breezes through the tutorial, you might direct them to a premade application library on your Oculus software and allow them to choose from a variety of applications.

Some Notes

- Some people feel more comfortable when you vocally guide them throughout the experience regarding what to expect or do during an interaction within the app. For others, too much talking will distract them or take them out of the experience. Use your best judgment.
- Clean equipment after each use.
- Ask permission or warn participants if you will need to touch them while assisting with the controls and VR gear.

RECOMMENDED NEXT PROJECTS

As you gain familiarity with offering these VR Explorations, it is important to:

- Gather resources and information from within your institution to direct your participants to the "next steps" if they want to explore the equipment more in the future, use it for gaming, or need consultations on how to include it in personal projects/research
- Engage with faculty and staff (in an academic setting) to encourage them to find ways to incorporate VR in their classrooms/jobs (considering a major goal of this program is exposure to library technologies)
- Find ways to partner in your community to potentially include introductory VR applications that were made by people in your community

Photogrammetry and Texture Baking
Creating Lightweight 3D Objects for Any VR Headset

SARAH HUBER, Engineering Technology Information Specialist
and Assistant Professor
ANDREW SUMNER, Visual Solutions Engineer
Purdue University, Indiana

P atrons will learn how to make 3D objects that are viewable across a range of consumer to high-end VR headsets through the processes of photogrammetry and texture baking. Photogrammetry is an afford-able and relatively simple process that recreates objects in 3D with great detail. The process includes taking photos of an object with a smartphone and then bringing them into open-source software that aligns them into what is called a point cloud. A point cloud is the first processing step in creating a 3D object. Point clouds can be complex and data-intensive; so, many consumer VR headsets do not have the capacity to render the objects for optimal viewing. Texture baking makes 3D objects "lightweight" in geometry for rendering, but the details are maintained using images for material properties. Lightweight 3D objects can be viewed across a range of VR headsets with stunning results. This activity includes three sections: (1) Photo Capture, (2) Photogrammetry Image Stitching, and (3) Texture Baking. Patrons will create 3D objects they can use for their video games, websites, artist portfolios, and more!

Age Range	Type of Library Best Suited For	Cost Estimate
Young adults (ages 13–18) Adults	Public libraries School libraries Academic libraries	$0–3,000 depending on equipment available

FIGURE 11.1 From photos to a 3D lightweight object

OVERVIEW

This guide walks patrons through the process of creating 3D objects from photos to be shown in VR/AR/the web. The instructions can be followed by individual patrons, but it is recommended that patrons work in small groups at least one time throughout the process. There are enough details to the process that patron collaboration through each section will be helpful. We recommend two to three separate workshops at a time length of two to three hours each to cover the topics: (1) Photo Capture, (2) Photogrammetry Image Stitching, and (3) Texture Baking. Due to the level of detail, patrons would benefit from an instructor working with each group.

Any digital camera that takes quality photos can be used for the photo-taking portion. For this activity, however, we focus on the use of smartphones because of affordability and access. Photogrammetry software "reconstructs" 3-dimensional models by comparing features between photos to align them into a 3D point cloud. Because the entire workflow relies on the quality of the photos taken, you should consider following some general rules (which we include below) to optimize the image capture.

For processing images in the photogrammetry and texture baking software, we include some specific troubleshooting suggestions. We encourage patrons to experiment with the troubleshooting options. Due to the state of the software, one set of prescribed directions across different scenarios limits successful 3D object creation. For this activity, we took photos of a lion sculpture on our university campus. Tutorial images referenced below can be found in a Dropbox folder at https://bit.ly/3gejFsy. If patrons want to select their image from a list of previously taken photos, the sculpture photos can be found in the same Dropbox folder.

NECESSARY EQUIPMENT AND MATERIALS

- Smartphone with the ability to take photos
- Desktop computer for processing (a Nvidia graphics card is required and is commonly included with the desktop)
- Dedicated graphics card (Nvidia); these are very common in desktop PCs and gaming-oriented laptops
  - Nvidia CUDA-enabled GPU (compute capability greater than or equal to 2.0)
- USB cable
- SD card reader
- Free, open-source software: Meshroom for photogrammetry and xNormal for texture baking

Recommended but Optional Materials

- If patrons do not have access to computers with dedicated graphics cards for Meshroom, MicMac is a less powerful, alternative software.
- Sketchfab for storing and viewing the published 3D object

STEP-BY-STEP INSTRUCTIONS

Preparation

- Install Meshroom and xNormal.

Photo Capture

- It is important for every image to have the same camera settings. For Android, select *Pro mode* (manual mode) to be able to set consistent ISO and shutter speeds between photos. For iPhone, consider purchasing the ProCamera app for the same purposes.
- Take approximately seventy-five photos in total. It is possible to make models from a few photos, but the quality typically will be low. For this project, try to choose an object you can walk around.
- Walk around the object 180 degrees, taking one photo at a time, trying to cover as much of the object in each photo as you can reach. For example,

take photos with the camera pointed straight on at the object and then try to take photos from above and below to cover the areas you cannot see from a more direct angle. Do not worry about covering areas similar to other photos you have taken—it is most important to get complete coverage around the point of interest.

- Coverage and consistency matter most in photogrammetry. The overlap between each photo should be thirty to fifty percent.
- Consider the following variables:
    - Lighting, reflections from shiny surfaces, and changes in camera settings will all cause inconsistencies in the data, which will cause difficulties with the software processing it as intended.
    - Objects with surfaces that are *not* reflective and well lit will be the easiest to scan.
- Once all the photos are taken, transfer them to a computer. This is easiest with a USB cable for phones or an SD card reader for cameras.

Photogrammetry Image Stitching in Meshroom

This section includes the most detail and has room for troubleshooting; so, it is important to give patrons time and help whenever needed.

- Install Meshroom.
- Orient yourself with the interface (See Image 1: Default Meshroom):
    - Images tab is on the left.
    - Image viewer is on the middle-left.
    - 3D Viewer is on the middle-right.
    - Graph Editor is on the bottom-left.
    - Node is on the bottom-right.
- Drag your photos into the *Images* column on the left (See Image 2: Added Images).
- Save the project using *File*, then *Save As*.
- Press the green *Start* at the top-center of the screen. Processing the images can take some time depending on the number of photos and their size. Expect longer processing times (greater than ten minutes) for image counts greater than fifty. In the Graph Editor at the bottom of the interface, you will find the nodes. When a node is complete, it turns green.
- Once the *StructureFromMotion Node* turns green, press *Stop* at the top of the screen. Then, you can click on that node to see the result of your

images being turned into a point cloud (See Image 3: StructureFrom-Motion Node).

- Click on the point cloud in the 3D Viewer. Rotate and pan around the object to assess the quality. If the point cloud looks good, move on to the process of *Decimation*. If the point cloud is a poor representation of your object, move to *Troubleshooting*.

- *Troubleshooting*: Stop the process (button at the top next to *Start*). Here are some Setting options to help you troubleshoot if needed:
  - In *FeatureExtraction*, you can change *Describer Preset* from *Normal* to *High*. This adds more detail to the process as the software looks for features in images to use for matching.
  - In *FeatureMatching*, enable *Guided Matching*. This adds a second stage to the matching process with new constraints based on the first stage for more accuracy.
  - In *StructureFromMotion*, increase the *minInputTrackLength* to three or four. This will only use the most accurate matches instead of attempting to include outliers (with some speed-up).
  - In *DepthMap*, reducing the *Nb Neighbour Cameras* (both *SGM* and *Refine*) can speed up processing by comparing fewer cameras for coverage of the same area. This one is heavily dependent on your coverage—more spread-out images can benefit from this.
  - In *Texturing*, reduce the *Texture Size* to 4096 and disable *Use UDIM*. This will use less overall resolution for the color information and take much less time to process.

- When the results are complete and the patron is satisfied with the object results, move on to *Decimation*. Remind patrons to save the project after processing.

- *Decimation*: Once the point cloud looks good, the polygon count will be very high. For example, in the case of the lion sculpture, the polygon count is over three million. To make a lightweight 3D object, take the following steps to make the polygon count smaller.
  - Patrons will use the *MeshDecimate node*; this will decimate or reduce the geometry to a specified amount. Patrons should decimate *before* texturing to apply the texture to this new lightweight mesh.
  - Click and drag the *Texturing node* further to the right in the Graph Editor and click and drag the *MeshFiltering node* down. This will give the patron room in the Graph Editor to easily see the node connections and provide space to add a node between *MeshFiltering* and *Texturing*.

- Disconnect the *MeshFiltering* output wire connected to *Texturing* by right-clicking on the wire and selecting *Remove*.
- Right-click in any open space in the Graph Editor to search for the *MeshDecimate node*. Select *MeshDecimate* to add it as a node.
- Connect the *MeshFiltering* to *MeshDecimate* with the output going to *inputMesh* on *Texturing*. Click and drag from the circles next to the output and input to connect the nodes together. The result will look like a white line has connected them.
- On *MeshDecimate*, set the *Max Vertices* to 50,000. This limits the total amount of vertices (and then faces). (See Image 4: MeshDecimate Node.)
- *Texturing:* A final step in reducing the polygon count within Meshroom is to *Texturize*.
  - Change the *Texture Size* to 2048. This lowers the output resolution of the texture.
  - Change the *Unwrap Method* to *LSCM* and ensure the settings match the recommendation in Section 2. *LSCM* will force the output texture to be a single image instead of splitting it up between many.
  - Deselect the *Use UDIM* checkmark. UDIMs are advanced workflow mods that enable the use of multiple texture maps for a single mesh, which is not ideal for VR applications. (See Image 5: Texturizing.)
- Once these nodes are set up, click the green *Start* again to process the mesh and decimation. Meshroom will compute any nodes that are not green to finish the process.

Texture Baking for Lightweight 3D Object in xNormal

Texture Baking: the process of "baking" information from a higher-resolution version of a mesh to a lower polygon version. Think of it as a high-to-low process during which the details from the high-quality versions are what will be saved into images to "fake" that information on top of a lower-resolution mesh.

- Download xNormal.
- Patrons can use xNormal to bake a *Normal Map*, which will fake depth in a texture to any rendering engine (Sketchfab, Unity, Unreal, etc.).

- For this process, patrons will need the high-quality mesh and the lower-quality mesh with texture. Right-click the *MeshFiltering node* and select *Open Folder* to find the high-quality mesh. Then right-click the *Texturing node* to find the lower-resolution mesh and the image texture.
- In xNormal, select the *High Definition Meshes* tab on the top-right.
- Drag and drop the high-definition model previously used (the *Mesh Filtering result folder*).
- Select *Low Definition Meshes* and drag the lower polygon mesh from the *Texturing output folder* from Meshroom.
- Select *Baking Options* and change the following settings (See Image 6: xNormalOptions):
  - Set the output file to a specific folder (click the 3-dot icon next to the text bar at the top), name the image, and change the format to jpg.
  - Change the size to 4096 × 4096 (lower if high-resolution details aren't required).
  - Check that *Normal Map* is selected.
  - Press *Generate Maps* in the bottom-right. The process will "render" the information to a blueish image.

Results

With this process, patrons can capture a physical object, compute a 3D reconstruction from it, and bake information from a high-detail form into a lightweight model capable of being rendered in any VR/AR/web application. The quickest way for patrons to use this model with the textures created for visualization is through Sketchfab, an online repository for browsing and uploading 3D models. Patrons should upload the mesh file and the two textures created—the color map and the normal map. With this platform, most VR headsets can view the models either through a web browser or Sketchfab's mobile application.

To export the finished creation, find the 3D model made in Meshroom by right-clicking the *Texturing node* and choosing *Open Folder*. Copy the .obj and the texture image to a location where you want to store your 3D model. Then, copy the resulting texture from the xNormal bake to the same location. These are now your finished model with a color texture and a normal texture.

RECOMMENDED NEXT PROJECTS

- Turntable photogrammetry: Objects are put on a lazy Susan, which rotates the object for the user as they take the photos as opposed to having patrons snap photos while walking around the object.
- Material scanning with photogrammetry: baking a surface scan to a material you could use on other digital objects.

Virtual Reality at Your Campus's Study Abroad Fair
Immersive Global Exploration Meets Library Outreach

LILIANA LAVALLE, Digital Learning and Instruction Librarian
McIntyre Library, University of Wisconsin–Eau Claire

T aking virtual reality equipment to your institution's study abroad fair provides students with a great opportunity to explore potential study abroad sites and offers an engaging outreach opportunity for your library. Using Google Earth VR, participants can immerse themselves—even if just for a few minutes—and take a virtual "walk" through campuses around the world. By displaying the user's VR view on a large, prominently located screen at the fair, you are not only helping to promote your school's study abroad programs but also boosting awareness of your library and its resources. VR technology allows an opportunity for casual, cost-free immersion, and it can serve as an icebreaker to open communication and build relationships between students, librarians, and study abroad staff. Students are excited to interact and share experiences with their peers and librarians when using VR. This event also allows librarians to connect with faculty and staff across campus to demonstrate library technology and teaching resources.

Age Range	Type of Library Best Suited For	Cost Estimate
Young adults (ages 13–18) Adults	School libraries Academic libraries	$0–$1,000

FIGURE 12.1 Exploring a potential study abroad site in Valparaíso, Chile, using street view in Google Earth VR

COST CONSIDERATIONS

If your library or school already has access to VR equipment, no other purchases are necessary, and staff time will be your only cost consideration for this program. Otherwise, purchasing new VR equipment could cost $1,000 (or more).

OVERVIEW

Helping students use VR at your campus's study abroad fair is more than just eye-catching entertainment; it benefits your students and your library. VR offers students a convenient low-stakes opportunity for global exploration. Students stay within their relative comfort zone while wandering through multiple worldwide destinations for free during lunch or a break between classes. VR allows students interested in study abroad (or those just curious about the world) to self-direct their own immersive, informal learning experience and discuss what interests them. This promotes meaningful interactions between peers, librarians, study abroad staff, and other mentors. While students are engaged with the VR program, librarians and study abroad staff can connect with them and enhance their experience by pointing out landmarks, giving directions, and answering questions as they naturally arise. VR removes travel boundaries and invites students to share their impressions and memories with others. Also, the VR view projected onto the "big screen" will inspire excitement and curiosity from participants and observers alike. During your conversations with students, you will encounter many opportunities to promote additional library services and materials.

Using VR applications in your institution's study abroad fair offers a flexible means of creating a program tailored to your specific event. To provide maximum visibility and accommodate the most participants, you will want to be present and facilitate the VR use for the entire duration of the fair. For a medium-sized crowd (our campus's study abroad fair is four hours long and attended by approximately eight hundred students), have at least two library staff members at the booth. Larger or longer fairs will require additional staff. For most of the fair, both staff members should engage with students (one by guiding the VR user, the other by conversing with crowd members and managing the waitlist). You will also appreciate the presence of a colleague to provide breaks during slower times. Both staff members will need to know how to operate and control your VR technology and instruct others on how to navigate the Google Earth VR software.

Keep in mind that VR technology causes motion sickness for many users. Let participants know this is a possibility as they put on the headset, and tell participants to remove the headset if they feel uncomfortable. I experience motion sickness when using VR software, and when I facilitated this program, I found that just watching the VR view on a screen could cause the same queasiness. Looking away or closing one's eyes reduces these effects but makes facilitating the program difficult or impossible. If you or one of your colleagues experiences VR-related motion sickness, arrange alternate or additional staffing for the event. Even if VR doesn't affect you negatively, be sensitive to the fact that some of your participants may experience motion sickness. Monitor participants for any distress, and always be ready to help them remove the headset if they mention dizziness, nausea, headaches, or feeling warm and sweaty. Have empty chairs nearby that do not face the screen so students can sit and recover as needed. While VR can be exciting and fun to many, please recognize and respect that it makes some of us very ill.

NECESSARY EQUIPMENT AND MATERIALS

- VR equipment (HTC Vive or Oculus Rift)
- A computer with Steam and Google Earth VR installed
- Tripods, extension cords, ethernet cables (the material you will need to set up your VR at another site)
- A projection screen or a monitor to display the VR user's view. A large and prominently placed screen at the front of the room is preferable
- Signage to indicate you are from the library (and about how students can access your VR technology)
- A waitlist: We used the low-tech option of paper and pencil and just called out people's names. You may want to enlist technology that can help you keep a waitlist of your participants.
- Sanitizing wipes or spray to disinfect the VR headset between users. You can swap out replacement foam face pads in your VR headset to make sanitizing easier.

STEP-BY-STEP INSTRUCTIONS

Preparation

- Build a partnership with your study abroad department or staff members who coordinate the fair. Suggest the inclusion of a VR "booth" and offer to facilitate this activity at the next fair. If colleagues are unsure how this would work, offer to demonstrate: Invite them to the library for a brief "show and tell" Google Earth VR session. In our case, this turned out to be a key step. Seeing what the technology could do in person convinced them not only to invite us to host a table at the fair, but they also featured the VR station at the front of the ballroom on the main projection screen and mentioned our VR program in their publicity materials. *Note:* If your study abroad fair offers any free food or beverage, see if it is possible for the library's VR booth to be located near those refreshment stands. Students enjoying free popcorn and lemonade with their friends are eager participants and a more patient audience, whereas a booth located near an entrance/exit may not have the same draw.
- Before the fair, create favorite locations in your Google Earth that correspond to your school's study abroad sites. Ask your study abroad

coordinator for a list of your current program locations and place your Google Earth favorites as close as possible to the center of your partner campuses. You can place favorites in the town centers instead, but we found that our students were much more eager to explore and revisit partner institutions' campuses.

- Arrive at the fair location well in advance to set up equipment and troubleshoot tech issues. Give yourself at least thirty extra minutes to set up your mobile VR system, test out display screens, and tape down cords. You will likely encounter some unforeseen snags: For us, it was internet connection issues.
- After running through the VR sensors' setup, tape or cordon off the floorspace where your VR users will be. Make sure there are no obstacles or tripping hazards in this area and place tables or signs to prevent others from accidentally wandering into this space.

Program Instructions

- Invite interested students near your booth to try out the library's VR system and explore a study abroad location. Students may be shy at first but opening with some casual conversation helps. Try asking students where they might want to study abroad or if they have ever tried VR before. If another student is using the VR, tell the other student(s) about the location that participant is exploring and ask if they'd like to try it out next.
- Briefly explain the headset and controllers and how to move around in Google Earth VR to the student before they begin. If the student has already used VR, this won't be necessary; even for those who have not, keep this intro very short. Usually, only a few seconds of preparation are needed when a user is putting on the headset. Students often learn the controls best by using them. Start the student's VR experience in the study abroad location they request using your preset favorite locations in Google Earth VR. Once the student has put on the headset, hand them the controllers and slowly walk them through the first few motions by watching their view on the screen and directing them to the correct buttons to push to move through Google Earth. They may need verbal or physical help locating and pressing buttons or adjusting their grip on the controllers; remember: they can't see you.

- Once the student can navigate independently, let them explore freely and strike up a conversation about what they are seeing. Encourage observation and let students take the lead to discuss buildings, people, nature . . . whatever interests them about the place they are viewing. Facilitate conversations between the participant and others (whom they cannot see and may not be able to hear clearly). You will notice that students who have studied abroad are eager to show their friends where they traveled, and study abroad staff are delighted to see students virtually exploring their sites. One program coordinator at our fair temporarily abandoned his booth in his excitement to give directions to the train station for a student wandering through his German hometown.

- The staff person who is not assisting the VR user should engage observers, manage the waitlist, and prepare additional participants. Having the next participant "on deck" is recommended to keep the line flowing smoothly. To further streamline the process during busy periods, the waitlist staff member can deliver a brief intro regarding the VR controls to the next user while they observe the current user. This allows the next person to seamlessly jump into the Google Earth VR app and navigate it more easily. If the waitlist includes more than a few people, you can advise students to check out some nearby booths and let them know you will call their name when it is their turn.

- Keep the VR user on track and keep things moving. Depending on the crowd, you may not need to restrict the students to specific places within Google Earth or keep strict time limits for sessions. This is recommended for larger crowds or if you have a constant waitlist of participants. When no one else was waiting, we encouraged students to check out multiple study abroad locations or even roam the globe freely. This can cause confusion for observers, though. For example, they might wonder why a student is viewing the Eifel Tower when your school has no study abroad sites in Paris. To avoid this issue, try to redirect students by suggesting they explore the nearest study abroad location leading to their point of interest. You can always encourage their natural curiosity (and plug library resources) by suggesting a future trip to the library VR lab to explore all the wonders of Google Earth at their leisure. When you have a waitlist, aim for five minutes or less per user so that a good number of people can experience the technology during the fair. Between users, sanitize the VR headset.

RECOMMENDED NEXT PROJECTS

Consider partnering further with your study abroad colleagues or faculty members who lead immersion trips. Google Earth VR can make for excellent pre- and post-trip activities. Are there places that faculty wish students could familiarize themselves with before they travel? Can students returning from study abroad lead virtual tours of some of their favorite places for other students? For students who cannot travel (for example, due to prohibitive costs, anxiety, family obligations, or the pandemic), VR equipment can offer an opportunity to explore the world at one's own pace for free without ever leaving campus. Think about how your VR technology can benefit all students through immersive experiences and get creative about potential campus partnerships. Your campus's language classrooms might use VR to practice giving directions, translate real-world signs, or analyze culture in public spaces. A hospitality class can create and present Google Earth virtual tours as a final class project.

As you encourage your students to explore the world through VR, consider exploring and experimenting regarding all the different/new ways VR can help students learn and connect with others. While virtual science labs and STEM applications are currently the more well-known uses of VR, academic libraries have numerous opportunities to expand VR's use in humanities and social sciences instruction. When you give students the opportunity to play with your library's VR equipment at outreach events, such as a study abroad fair or during their classes, you are building awareness of library resources and engaging, entertaining, and educating your audience all at the same time.

VR for All
A STEM Library Engineers Open House

ELIZABETH P. WAUGH, Virtual and Distance Learning Initiatives Librarian
JESSICA URICK OBERLIN, Information Technology Initiatives Librarian
Pennsylvania College of Technology

ntroducing a virtual reality space at your institution may seem daunting; however, hosting a VR open-house event can provide a fun and budget-friendly introduction to your new VR space. Given its limitless applications, VR can be implemented into many STEM-based courses from health sciences and medicine to architecture and engineering. A VR open-house event is a great way to jumpstart interest in VR and highlight your library's resources. This VR open-house program targets educators and students in STEM classes specifically—both groups can benefit from this event. Educators can observe firsthand the different application offerings and how those apps can be integrated into their courses. Students will have the opportunity to use VR, possibly for the first time, and discover uses for this emerging technology for classwork and recreation. Hosting a VR open house is a surefire way to spark interest, spread awareness, and implement a fun and fresh VR space. In addition, this program provides information on how to create, promote, and maintain a VR library space that can be used and enjoyed by all at your institution.

Age Range	Type of Library Best Suited For	Cost Estimate
Young adults (ages 13–18) Adults	School libraries Academic libraries	$80–$7,100

COST CONSIDERATIONS

While the upper range of the cost estimate may appear high, it includes the potential cost of the creation of your entire VR space. This cost estimate includes the purchase of the VR equipment for the room: the headset, controllers, monitors, computer, and cleaning supplies. The program and VR studio will serve an educational purpose, and a higher initial purchase price ensures inclusion of the most current VR technology. Another consideration to note is that VR is a quickly developing technology, and the VR equipment will need to be updated every three to five years.

Despite the high-cost estimate when first creating a VR space, some expenses can be spared if the VR equipment has already been purchased. The open-house costs would then be limited to refreshments and the purchase of a few additional tools: a whiteboard and dry erase markers. In addition, purchasing a kit to adapt the headsets to a wireless format may be warranted but is not essential. Another variable is the number of screens needed for the space. One monitor will suffice, but a second may be required to see the user in action if your space has no windows. The second monitor, mounted outside the VR space, would allow staff members to monitor the gameplay to ensure user safety and enable classmates, teachers, and friends to view the gameplay too. Depending on your space and the equipment you need to purchase, the cost estimate for the open house can vary greatly.

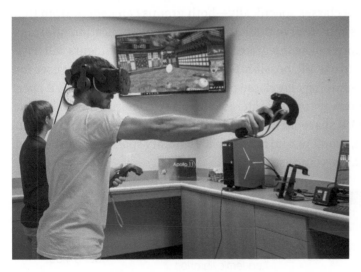

FIGURE 13.1
Students using the Madigan Library/ Pennsylvania College of Technology VR Studio; photo courtesy of Pennsylvania College of Technology

OVERVIEW

The VR open-house program is designed to implement VR into your institution by introducing VR to students who may or may not have experienced it before and to educators interested in incorporating VR in their curriculum and courses. This open-house format is intended to be driven by STEM interests and majors including but not limited to gaming, gaming simulation, computing, physician assistance, architecture, electrical technology, and/or other IT fields. The event and program will show educators and students how they can incorporate VR into both recreational and educational uses for various STEM careers and programs. Due to the nature of this exciting hands-on program, expect a relatively large group to sign up. Having an attendance cap is recommended depending on your available space and the number of staff members involved in the program. Always include information for those who attend but did not get the chance to experience the full VR session; ensure they are aware of the space's hours of availability and have clear expectations regarding the use of the equipment and space.

Time allotment for the program should be around two hours. Expect a variety of questions and ensure that those who monitor the gameplay during the program are positive, encouraging, and knowledgeable and are able to answer questions in a way that encourages growth and participation. An ideal program would call for a minimum of three staff members trained in using your headset and the different VR applications so that they will understand how the apps complement and align with specific majors, classes, and programs. You can also collaborate with various personnel, such as ITS staff or instructional technology staff, who can assist in hosting your event.

Your VR open-house program should follow a simple and engaging format. Beginning with a speech briefly explaining VR technology, most of the program will consist of attendees trying the VR technology in short segments. To accommodate and engage the attendees waiting to play, assign one staff member to answer their questions and pass out more information. Also, using a whiteboard and dry erase markers, participants can be encouraged to write suggestions for improvement or ideas for the space. After the initial open-house program, your VR studio can hold limited hours and have a checkout procedure for the space. Gamers can use this designated area if a qualified staff member or student worker is on hand to monitor all gameplay to ensure player safety and proper equipment usage. Your open-house program can spread awareness about your VR space by bolstering user confidence, providing information for further research, and enabling your students to use VR independently.

NECESSARY EQUIPMENT AND MATERIALS

- Promotional materials: posters, flyers, and/or bookmarks as well as online content promoting the upcoming open-house event
- HTC Vive Pro headset and controllers
- Alienware Aurora PC
- Two 4K 55-inch monitors: one inside the room and one outside of it for staff to oversee the activities and for attendees to view the gameplay
- Viveport and Steam VR (pre-installed)
- Cleaning materials/supplies to clean the headset:
  - Antibacterial wipes to sanitize the headset and controllers
  - Microfiber cleaning cloths to clean the lens on the headset

Recommended but Optional Materials

- LibGuide or a dedicated website to showcase the VR studio's hours and resources as well as the books, articles, and databases in your library's collection
- Wireless adapter kit for the HTC Vive Headset
- Whiteboard, dry erase markers, and an easel that can be accessed from a standing position
- Refreshments for attendees (be mindful of placement away from your equipment and VR space)

Note: All materials should be compliant with accessibility standards and accommodations.

STEP-BY-STEP INSTRUCTIONS

Preparation

- Schedule a photo op or record a video of someone using the equipment, such as your college's president, your school's principal, or another well-known figure, to use in the promotional materials.

- Create promotional materials to advertise your VR space and open-house event.
- Post advertisements physically and on any social media accounts.
- Purchase VR and instructional resources for your library's collections including eBooks and journals.
- Create a LibGuide or website containing VR resources for educators and students, hours and procedures, and any other information about your space.
- Train staff on technology, safety measures, and how VR connects to programs and majors.
- Purchase cleaning supplies.
- Arrange for refreshments and setup of your VR equipment, whiteboard, and refreshment tables.
- Formally invite educators and students from specific subject areas or classes to attend the event.

Engage

- Start the program with a roughly fifteen-minute speech that introduces VR technology to your audience and gives a brief tour of the VR studio.
  - The speech should ensure that those who are unfamiliar with VR will be able to understand what the program is about and what technology is being used.
  - The initial speech will give you the opportunity to tell your audience the purpose of your VR studio: to create a space to enhance the student experience in and out of class.
- After your opening speech, ask your attendees if they are willing to volunteer to try the VR technology.
- Start demonstrations slowly and answer questions about the VR Studio in a positive way.
- Connect VR applications and games to students' classes.
- Create a positive atmosphere by allowing trial and error so that attendees will be excited to participate.
- Encourage questions throughout the gameplay.
- While one player is using the headset, another knowledgeable staff member or two can answer questions, show VR equipment, and hand out brochures to keep the other attendees engaged and informed.

- Depending on the equipment used in the demonstrations, your staff members can bring out pieces of technology and show them to the attendees waiting in line so that everyone can see the technology even if they do not have the chance or desire to play.
- Provide brochures with links or QR codes to your VR studio's web page or LibGuide that contain the space's hours, books in your catalog, specific databases that contain information on VR, and student and faculty resources.

Explore

- Demonstrate the games and applications using the headset, room, and monitors.
- Assist the players so that they properly wear the headset and use the controllers.
- Provide the attendees the opportunity to try your VR headset during the open house under the supervision of one of your staff members.
  - Depending on your available space, your VR studio could be set up in a room that contains the headset and controllers, the computer, and a large monitor to view gameplay. A second monitor can be placed outside of the VR studio so that gameplay can be monitored by a staff member while ensuring that the users have their own space.
  - If your VR studio room is small, one option for your open house would be to have one staff member, one attendee, and a friend or two enter the VR studio while the rest of the attendees remain outside and watch the gameplay on the outside monitor.
  - Time slots of five to seven minutes of gameplay are recommended for the open house demonstrations.
- Ask the users what classes they are taking or what they are interested in playing so that patrons can choose a game that suits their interests.
- Use the gameplay as a means of instruction and use the player as an example of how to use VR, either correctly or incorrectly, so the audience can learn and be a part of the gameplay.
- Highlight the subject-specific games and applications available to educators to benefit their classes.

Empower

- Provide handouts with links to your LibGuide or website and additional materials in the catalog so users can research an area of VR that interests them or broaden their overall knowledge of VR.
- Provide usage instructions for users of all levels so that everyone feels confident that they can use VR successfully.
- Create promotional brochures to showcase specific majors so students can make the connection between the VR Studio and their majors/career path.
- Include informational materials specifically geared toward VR for educators including educational websites and instructional resources your library can access.
- Show players that they have support, their questions will be answered, and they will not be judged based on experience.
- Highlight web pages that contain VR studio hours so that users know when they can use the studio.
- Show users access points and how they can use the VR space during the academic year after the open house ends.
- Set up a whiteboard on an easel with dry erase markers where your audience can write down suggestions for the VR studio. Suggestions can range from:
  - Applications and games to purchase
  - How to improve the studio's physical setup
  - Other potential VR programs they would like to attend
  - Ways to improve how you teach VR to students

LEARNING OUTCOMES

Students and faculty will:

- Apply correct VR safety measures and equipment usage
- Understand how VR applies to the professional world and to specific subjects and majors
- Improve and use their VR skills to become independent users
- Receive information on VR and library resources for further research

- Gain insight into new VR technology offerings
- Receive answers to their questions and know who to contact with questions about VR in the future

RECOMMENDED NEXT PROJECTS

Now that your VR open house has launched VR at your institution, you can sustain the momentum by holding major or subject-specific events. You could choose to focus on one subject area per month using specific applications. Library or IT staff can send follow-up correspondences asking educators for feedback on the open house and offering ideas on how to incorporate VR into their subject areas. This will enable you and your staff to stay current regarding new and developing applications and games, which will give your students more experience using VR.

For example, November is National Alzheimer's Disease Awareness Month in the United States. During that month, you could create a program that uses a VR dementia simulator and that specifically benefits premed, health sciences, or nursing students. You could promote the program by hanging posters around campus, advertising over social media, and creating a display with your collection's resources on dementia, Alzheimer's, and other geriatric conditions. Your program could be open to all students and instructors, but you could specifically invite health science, premed, or nursing students to your VR Studio to use the VR dementia simulators. This basic formula could be used for engineering students learning to create 3D models of their projects, architecture students "visiting" famous landmarks, and graphic design students "touring" famous museums—all by using VR.

Another suggestion would be to keep a record of statistics regarding the use of the VR space from the open house into your academic year. You could keep a simple record of overall use broken down by time frames to accommodate users in the future, especially during heavily trafficked times, or break it down further by keeping track of subject areas in your institution that may need more resources or instructors who may need help in learning how to use the VR space. It's VR for all who use your fun and educational space after an inviting and helpful open-house event.

VR on Wheels
Bring the Virtual World to Your Audience

ALVARO ALVAREZ, **Innovative Media Librarian**
University of California, Riverside

magine a world where you could slay dragons, go on magical quests, or create an art piece from nothing in mid-air. Thanks to virtual reality, your target audience can immerse themselves in these magical places and create like never before. Most libraries are limited in space; this project can help alleviate this problem by providing a portable service that your audience will love. The VR cart can be a very versatile tool you can use to learn, teach, and have fun with by picking any of the thousands of games or apps that cover educational topics in a fun way available via this technology. When you are finished using the cart, cleanup will be easy, and you can store it almost anywhere such as a small closet or an office corner.

Age Range	Type of Library Best Suited For	Cost Estimate
Tweens (ages 8–12) Young adults (ages thirteen through eighteen) Adults	Public libraries School libraries Academic libraries	$3,000–$3,500

COST CONSIDERATIONS

The cost is based on the quality of the items you purchase. For example, you can purchase a PC with the basic specifications needed to run VR, or you can choose one that is higher quality. Also, the quality of the cart will have a significant impact on the cost.

OVERVIEW

This portable VR program can be a very versatile way to explore and share this new innovative technology. Use of the cart will allow you to bring the VR experience to your audience in almost any setting. One issue libraries have is space, and with this cart, you will be able to move your equipment from area to area and store it very easily. The setup is fast and simple.

The cart can be utilized in a variety of ways. It can be incorporated into events, lesson plans, and fun activities; checked out by patrons for use within the library; or used for demo purposes. Some examples of uses for the cart are:

- To facilitate a de-stress event in your library—you can set up the cart and allow patrons to use it for five minutes each to get their minds off studying and to enjoy some entertainment.
- To allow classes to easily learn about their courses in an academic library setting—each student can take a turn using the VR cart, and because

FIGURE 14.1
Portable VR cart high-end virtual reality experience for class instruction and recreational and outdoor library events.

the cart has a TV, everyone in the class will be engaged while individual students use the equipment.

- For students or faculty wanting to learn about VR development or conducting research around the subject matter—they can visit the library and set up a time to use the cart in the building.
- For class integration—students can be assigned to use the VR cart for class projects, research, or extra credit.
- For clubs and other organizations on campus who wish to host a VR night, game night, freshman orientation, and so forth.
- For department training such as safety procedures regarding earthquakes or fires.

Staffing requirements for the cart are minimal; one or two people can handle it. It only requires a quick setup and monitoring during usage to ensure safety and proper use of the equipment. The setup is fast—taking approximately five minutes—and the cleanup, which takes about the same amount of time as setup, consists only of booting up/shutting down the equipment and setting up/taking down the sensors on the tripods. If you plan on allowing patrons to check out the cart within your building, you will need to train them on the proper usage of the equipment and ask them to sign a checkout agreement so that they will be accountable in case of any damage. If possible, have a staff member monitor them while they use it, and make sure you have a safe area or room that it can be set up in.

NECESSARY EQUIPMENT AND MATERIALS

- One HTC Vive Pro headset
- TV cart stand with a cabinet to store extra equipment
- 32- to 43-inch TV
- Tripods
- VR-ready PC
- Surge protector for multiple devices

Recommended but Optional Materials

- HTC Vive wireless adapter
- HTC Vive wireless adapter attachment kit
- Double-sided tape
- Zip ties for cables
- Power extension cables if outlets are far away from your desired setup locations

STEP-BY-STEP INSTRUCTIONS

Preparation

Have all necessary equipment and materials ready to begin building the cart.

- Add VR sensors to the tripods.
- Add the TV to the cart.
- Add the surge protector to the cart (use double-sided tape to mount it).
- Add the computer to the cabinet (attach the computer's base to the cabinet using double-sided tape to stabilize the computer if you wish).
- Connect the HTC Vive, computer, and TV (use zip ties to help organize the cables if you wish).
- Follow the HTC Vive instructions for your VR setup.
- Determine which apps you would like to buy and download (some are free).

Program Instructions

- Boot up the PC and power on the HTC Vive.
- Make sure the HTC Vive is connected to the PC.
- Plug in the sensors.
- Follow the HTC Vive room setup instructions to add boundaries for user safety.
- Launch the app.
- Help users put on the headset and hand the two VR controllers to them.
- To clean up, shut down your computer and unplug the sensors.
- Store everything in the cabinet and wheel it back to its storage area.

RECOMMENDED NEXT PROJECTS

- Add VR to a multipurpose room by mounting the sensors to a wall and then wheel in the cart when needed.
- Host workshops on how to create VR apps and games using the cart to demo your lesson.

Virtual Reality as a Medium for Community Art

ANNA MAULDIN SPETH, Librarian for Emerging Technology and Digital Projects
Pepperdine University, California

This program employs virtual reality as the medium for a community art piece. VR gives artists an opportunity to create an immersive world that exceeds the possibilities of our real one. VR community art is a highly customizable program that can be administered as a stand-alone initiative or in partnership with other events. You can create an immersive environment and engage community members through exploration and transformation of the environment based on a question or theme.

Engaging your patrons through collaborative art can enrich dialogue between the library and the community, create a sense of belonging, document community history, and so much more. As a platform, VR encourages participants to experiment with an emerging technology, which can promote agency and reflection regardless of the participant's prior technical experience. Participants learn a new skill and feel empowered to incorporate VR into their own creative endeavors. This will drive interest in using VR, which serves as a promotion for all the VR technology available at your library.

Age Range	Type of Library Best Suited For	Cost Estimate
Young adults (ages 13–18) Adults	Public libraries School libraries Academic libraries	$500–$3000

COST CONSIDERATIONS

Program costs vary depending on the availability of technology and expertise at your institution. For example, if you already have VR hardware, the cost could be as low as $19.99 for the Tilt Brush app. Alternatively, if you purchase VR hardware and supply a stipend for a VR artist to facilitate the program, the event could cost thousands of dollars. Even if you need to purchase new equipment, you can choose from a wide variety of hardware that supports this program.

OVERVIEW

In this program, participants explore an immersive environment created in the Tilt Brush app and contribute to it based on a theme or question. This program involves intense preparation but is highly customizable. You will need to identify a theme, create an immersive environment using Tilt Brush, and practice leading participants through VR use. No prior VR experience is required to run this program.

Tilt Brush is a very easy-to-use, beginner-friendly drawing application made by Google. It works well as an introduction to VR but also has the tools necessary to create a highly detailed immersive environment. Constructing the environment for this event is a great way to become more familiar and comfortable with VR.

During the event, you will need at least one staff member available at all times to assist participants with the technology. The program can run any-where from a couple of hours to several weeks, depending on your staffing availability and the nature of the event. Only one participant can use a VR headset at a time, which does create a bottleneck, but other participants frequently find watching the person using the program engaging. There is a limit, however, to how long people will wait to use the headset; so, a drop-in setting or running this program in conjunction with another event works best.

Once the program is complete, the final piece can be saved locally to view using the institution's headsets or exported and shared as still images, as a video, or as 3D files.

NECESSARY EQUIPMENT AND MATERIALS

This program requires a headset, a monitor capable of showing what the participant sees in the headset, and a copy of Tilt Brush. Several hardware configurations will work with this program.

Option 1: Tethered Headset (Recommended)

- One tethered VR headset compatible with Tilt Brush (HTC Vive, Oculus Rift, Windows Mixed Reality, Valve Index, PlayStation VR)
- Tilt Brush app
- Computer capable of running a VR headset
- Instructional poster
- Masking tape

Option 2: All-in-one headset

- One Oculus Quest headset
- Tilt Brush software
- A television and Google Chromecast
- Instructional poster
- Masking tape

STEP-BY-STEP INSTRUCTIONS

Preparation

- Ensure the VR headset is operating correctly and running Tilt Brush.
- A *note on hardware*: During the event, participants not actively using the headset should be able to see what the person in the headset is doing on a monitor. This feed will help you instruct the participant in the headset, give participants who are nervous about VR more confidence through a real-time demonstration, keep the crowd engaged, and foster dialogue about different interpretations of your theme or question. With a tethered headset, this functionality is built into the traditional setup. If you are using an Oculus Quest, setup will be more involved. The Oculus Quest is capable of casting to a TV using Google Chromecast. However,

the cast will end if no one uses the headset for a few minutes, requiring a staff member to put on the headset and restart the cast. This can be tedious and disrupts the flow of the event. I recommend using a tethered headset if possible.

- Identify a theme or topic for your community artwork.
- Enlist someone to create the immersive environment. This person does not need to have VR experience but an artistic inclination does help. Tilt Brush is a beginner-friendly app, and this can be a chance for someone to gain experience with the medium. This person can be yourself, a colleague, a student worker, a volunteer, or a paid artist depending on your budget and staff availability.
- Involve the artist in conversations with those running the event to figure out the best way to bring your theme to life. Be sure to address the following before you begin creating the immersive environment:
  - How will participants contribute to the piece? Are they answering a specific question? Reacting to a theme, statement, or event? Are they bound to a certain area of the piece?
  - How will participants physically interact with the piece? Will they be walking? Standing? Seated? Is it viewable by users with a range of physical abilities? Is the height appropriate for all participants? Do they need a chair that spins?
  - Note: I recommend avoiding creating a piece that requires the teleport function to explore the program. Teaching new VR users how to teleport adds frustration and can make the participant less likely to enjoy the experience. Additionally, resetting the piece to its original starting point between users breaks the flow of the event and can be a point of irritation for the facilitator.
  - How much physical space is needed to explore the piece? If using a tethered headset, how will the tether be managed?
- Create a poster or other visual aid with simple, clear instructions on how to contribute to the piece. VR still has a high intimidation factor for many new users, and though people may stop to watch other people using the headset, many may remain uncertain about trying it. Create a poster that has clear, concise steps so participants understand exactly what contributing entails. Make sure it is visible to everyone at the event. Also, devise a clear script for you or your staff to use when facilitating the event.

- If using an Oculus Quest, ensure that your Quest is capable of casting to a screen using Chromecast. I found that I could not successfully cast over our institutional network but solved this issue by using a hotspot.
- Test everything in advance! Ask colleagues less familiar with VR to go through the entire process the same way your participants will. Use the poster and script. Identify points of confusion or frustration and edit as needed. Using VR for the first time can be a big ask, and users testing the experience to ensure it is enjoyable is a critical step.

Day of Setup

- If you are setting up VR in a different location than usual, leave plenty of time (at least an hour—ideally more) for troubleshooting.
- Tape off the boundary on the floor. People using the headset are blind to the real world; so, the tape will be a reminder to those not in the headset to give the participant space.
- Set up the poster and computer monitor (if using a tethered headset) or the TV and Chromecast (if using Quest).
- Load the prepared artwork.

During the Event

- Facilitate user additions to the artwork. When helping participants, the facilitator should remember that the user is blind to the outside world and always inform and ask permission before they touch the user or the headset. For example, you could say, "I'm going to adjust the Velcro straps on the headset to make it fit better. Is that okay?"
- The facilitator should monitor the contributions for any inappropriate material. This was something I was concerned about while hosting this event with undergraduates, but it did not end up being an issue. However, you should have a conversation beforehand about the suitability of asking participants to censor their contributions for your particular event and how to handle the situation if it does arise.
- Save the work frequently during the event.

Saving and Sharing the Final Product

Tilt Brush sketches can be saved locally, published to Google Poly (accessible by other Tilt Brush users or online), or exported in various formats (GIF, video, or screenshots) using the camera function built into the Tilt Brush menu. Detailed documentation of the process for each of these options is available online.

RECOMMENDED NEXT PROJECTS

Now that you've mastered creating immersive worlds and engaging new users with VR technology, so many projects are open to you! Enthusiastic participants may return to use the device to create their own VR artwork. Explore chapter 3: "Sculpting in VR: Using Oculus Rift + Medium," or chapter 20: "Designing in Virtual Reality: Using Apps to Create and Make," for further ways to support them. You can also pursue ways to present your community art piece and patron creations through creating a VR art exhibit. See chapter 21: "How to Create a VR Art Exhibition," or chapter 4: "Leveraging VR Software to Create Virtual Art Exhibitions."

Augmented Reality Introduction for Libraries
Metaverse and Library Services

PLAMEN MILTENOFF, Information Specialist
St. Cloud State University, Minnesota

n this project, faculty and/or staff from a public or academic library will enable patrons to actively participate in the delivery of library services. The use of Metaverse as an augmented reality (AR) addition to current library services will empower patrons to acquire information and build on their own knowledge regarding basic library services, thus enabling library personnel to conserve time and energy that they can then dedicate to more complex tasks and services. Metaverse has amassed popularity as an AR tool in K12, a fact that can prove useful when planning for students' transition from K12 to a higher-education environment. Familiarity with technological tools and platforms has always been a valuable component of student success. Metaverse facilitates gamification of the learning process and presents an opportunity for data collection. Such data can be incorporated into a larger Internet-of-Things (IoT) environment, assist in the application of artificial intelligence, and ultimately help to streamline and improve personalized learning.

Age Range	Type of Library Best Suited For	Cost Estimate
Young adults (ages 13–18) Adults This program is suggested for college-age students.	Public libraries Academic libraries	$500 (if the organization's smartphone is needed for testing or lending)

OVERVIEW

In this project, librarians will work with library student workers and patrons on transitioning traditional (paper-based and/or electronic) handouts (e.g., for policies) and tutorials into gamified AR documents and tutorials. In addition to ubiquitously accessible electronic formats, tutorials built using Metaverse AR will empower patrons to use their phones in much the same way as Pokémon GO excited millions of users around the world. Whether your tutorials are geared toward library student workers or for instructing library patrons on the usage of library services and/or other library-related functions, student workers and patrons can use their phones to navigate through the physical spaces of the library as well as learn about library services and concepts. AR, the ability to superimpose virtual content over accepted reality, is a promising new trend based on the principles of constructivism. While Metaverse is limited in its ability to create AR content, the advantage of the platform, compared to more advanced tools, such as Unity, is its WYSIWYG interface; the creator of the content does not have to be a programmer and/or have coding skills. Metaverse is a drag-and-drop application, which allows the Metaverse operator to incorporate media-rich tutorials (including 360-degree videos and still images) and gamify the experience for the end-user.

NECESSARY EQUIPMENT AND MATERIALS

- A Metaverse Studio account (free): https://studio.gometa.io/discover/me
- A relatively up-to-date smartphone

Recommended but Optional Materials

- A 360-degree camera if you wish to incorporate 360 videos and images

STEP-BY-STEP INSTRUCTIONS

- Create a Metaverse Studio account.
- Create the experience(s) (Metaverse Studio calls its projects "experiences").
- Explore the options available in the first scene. Watch YouTube tutorials to familiarize yourself with the logic of Metaverse and the opportunities of the platform.
- If you have not already done so, once you familiarize yourself with Metaverse's capabilities, create the screenplay for your project (in Metaverse language: experience).
- Prepare the materials you will be using for your Metaverse experience: e.g., policies, directions, exercises, regular and 360-degree images/ videos, and so forth.
- Develop the scenes and test using Metaverse Studio. Apply changes and improvements.
- Test using the Metaverse app on your phone. Apply changes and improvements.
- Share with a pilot group of friends and colleagues and ask them to test using Metaverse apps on their phones. Make sure you have as diverse a pilot group as possible in terms of smartphones with different operating systems: e.g., iOS and Android.
- Roll out the Metaverse experience, preferably first with your student workers, and then poll them to gain feedback regarding content and usability.

Engage

- An excellent approach for using Metaverse for instructional purposes for both student workers at the library and patrons of the library is to gamify the AR experience. For example, student workers can play a "scavenger hunt" that entails re-shelving books into stacks.
- The supervisor develops the "hoops" the student worker needs to "jump through" according to the regular tasks associated with book shelving.

- The supervisor can assign "quizlike" questions for complex situations to jumpstart each student worker's critical thinking connected with the book-shelving tasks.
- The supervisor can include 360-degree panoramas of difficult areas in the library to improve the student worker's library orientation.
- A short survey at the end of the game can harvest feedback from the student workers to assess the success of the current scavenger hunt and collect student ideas to improve the engagement through other/additional gamification techniques.
- Similar scavenger-hunt experiences can be created for library orientation and library instruction for novice patrons.
- Metaverse can be successfully used to also create "escape room" experiences.

Explore

The scavenger hunt program can be further developed to encourage students to explore information/materials on their own to increase their information/digital literacy as well as their familiarity with additional services in the library.

Empower

Metaverse AR content is explicitly directed toward enabling students to develop knowledge and skills as independently as possible. Gamifying library orientation and instruction with Metaverse AR and conducting sessions in groups of two or a maximum of three people allow peer learning and support, as per Vygotsky, and develop team-building and collaborative skills.[1] Well-structured Metaverse content offers gentle support and direction to students while also giving them a clear sense of ownership of the process, thus developing their confidence and self-reliance.

Learning Outcomes

Participants will:

- Learn the basic concept of AR—library faculty and staff who create the Metaverse content used in the program will be able to apply and/or use AR techniques in learning, teaching, and acquiring new skills.

- Become familiar with AR techniques, thus enabling patrons to learn and acquire new skills.

RECOMMENDED NEXT PROJECTS

Metaverse Studio's minimal cost presents multiple opportunities for simple AR projects. This software can be used as a means of introduction to AR. Building a project and creating a Metaverse experience is an excellent start, potentially leading to more complex and high-end projects involving considerably more expensive gear such as Microsoft HoloLens, Magic Leap, and similar software. Moreover, the exposure to an AR project with Metaverse introduces librarians, student workers, and patrons to the intricacies of this new technology and, respectively, teaches project organizers skills that help them manage structure, projects, manpower, and so forth, which will be indispensable during any later transitions to higher-end projects.

If your Metaverse library projects receive a strong welcome and support among patrons and student workers, the next step could involve collaborative Metaverse experiences based on content developed by librarians and faculty from different disciplines; e.g., development of an escape room for students (which would tap into their physics major, including information literacy elements from that field). Similarly, your library could become part of a campus-wide scavenger hunt new students can participate in to acquaint them with campus offices and services. Such a collaborative scavenger hunt can introduce students to rapidly advancing technology, strengthen retention, and increase the opportunity for successful learning outcomes.

NOTE
1. "Lev Vygotsky," Wikipedia, https://en.wikipedia.org/wiki/Lev _Vygotsky.

Activities for Calcflow Virtual Reality Software Exploring Vector Operations in Virtual Reality

GAVIN MEIGHAN, Library Student Worker

LINDA BURROW, Information Systems Specialist II

DOROTHY OGDON, Emerging Technologies Librarian

University of Alabama at Birmingham Libraries

C alcflow is a freely available virtual reality software for head-set-mounted displays (HMDs) such as the Oculus Rift and HTC Vive. Calcflow leverages the immersive nature of 3D virtual environments to provide a tool for developing a spatially based understanding of concepts from calculus. This chapter provides sets of practice activities to help participants begin using Calcflow to explore vector operations. Three-dimensional concepts, as described in calculus, can be challenging for new learners. Calcflow provides a low-pressure environment for young adults and older adults to begin hands-on virtual exploration of advanced concepts using guided learning in these activities. Only a basic knowledge of vector operations is needed prior to working through these activities. Each set of activities is designed to be completed by pairs of learners and works best when used with an HMD mirrored to a two-dimensional display.

Age Range	Type of Library Best Suited For	Cost Estimate
Young adults (ages 13–18) Adults	School libraries Academic libraries	$2,000–$3,000 or $5

COST CONSIDERATIONS

The costs for this program will vary greatly depending on whether the library has already purchased either an HTC VIVE or Oculus Rift headset and a VR-ready computer workstation. The cost above reflects an estimated purchase cost for one wired HMD, a VR-capable computer, and an additional display.

If the library already has access to a compatible HMD and VR-ready computer, the cost of this program will equal only the cost of the paper printouts needed for the program.

OVERVIEW

In this program, participants will be introduced to concepts in vector operations using tools in the VR software, Calcflow. Calcflow, a freely available VR software developed by Nanome, Inc., is available for the HTC VIVE and Oculus Rift but is not yet available for the Oculus Quest. Calcflow can be downloaded from the Nanome website (https://nanome.ai/calcflow), Steam, or Vive Port. In this chapter, we use three sets of activities focused on vector operations: Vectors I: placing vectors and plotting points in three-dimensional space; Vectors II: adding vectors in three-dimensional space; and Vectors III: the cross product, for participants to use during the program. These vectors activities were prepared and tested by Gavin Meighan, an undergraduate student at the University of Alabama at Birmingham majoring in mechanical engineering, and Linda Burrow, Library Information Systems specialist. Each set of activities is available from our library guide and a shared folder in UAB Box, one of our university's institutional cloud storage solutions. The activities are formatted as handouts and are available as PDF files.

In each vectors activity, one participant is the reader who is assigned to read the written activity to a wearer—a participant actively using the HMD to follow the instructions in Calcflow. Vectors I, II, and III guide users through describing and understanding vector operations in Calcflow. This prepares the program participants to explore calculus concepts independently within VR and lays a foundation for self-guided learning as a supplement to structured academic activities. Allow an hour to an hour and a half for both participants to work together through a vectors activity and then have them trade roles if desired. This program can be delivered as three separate sessions (one for each vectors activity) on multiple days or as a single day with breaks planned between sessions.

These instructions assume the library has access to an HMD attached to a VR-ready computer with internet access. The HMD should be mirrored to an external display, enabling the reader to view the activities of the wearer. If using multiple HMDs for this program, we recommend assigning one staff member for every two HMDs in use during the program to provide support and troubleshooting, especially if program participants are new to HMD-based VR.

NECESSARY EQUIPMENT AND MATERIALS

- At least one HTC Vive or Oculus Rift HMD with output mirrored to an external two-dimensional monitor or similar digital display
- Calcflow software
- Two printed copies of the Vectors I, Vectors II, or Vectors III activities for each workstation to be used during the session
- A pen or pencil for the reader to use to fill in blanks and make notes

Recommended but Optional Materials

- External storage device for transferring screenshots to cloud-based storage, external storage (such as a flash drive), or printing on a two-dimensional, paper-based printer
- A pen or pencil for recording information on the printed activity sheets

STEP-BY-STEP INSTRUCTIONS

Preparation

At least one day before the program begins:

- Download and install Calcflow on the workstation(s) to be used with the HMD(s) for the program.

- Print one set of instructions for Vectors I, Vectors II, or Vectors III for each HMD to be used for the program. PDF copies of the vectors activities can be downloaded from this shared folder: https://uab.box.com/v/uablib calcflow and are also available on the handouts page of our VR library guide: https://guides.library.uab.edu/VR/handouts.
- Have all library employees supporting HMD use during the program complete the activity in both the reader and wearer role before the program begins.

One hour before the program begins:

- Turn on and test all HMDs to be used for the program.
- Launch and test Calcflow.
- Distribute two printed copies of the selected vectors activity to each workstation.

Program Instructions

- Have the participants pair off or assign pairs and guide participants to their assigned HMD.
- Have the participants decide who will be the first wearer and the first reader.
- Have the first wearer put on and adjust the HMD.
- Have the reader begin working through the activity with the wearer.
- Once the wearer has completed the activity, have the participants switch roles.

RECOMMENDED NEXT PROJECTS

After completing the three vectors activities, users will be able to use Calcflow independently to demonstrate vector operations. Participants interested in additional activities in Calcflow may consider using the program's collection of predefined volumetric shapes to create customized objects that can be exported in .STL format for 3D printing.

Amazin' Creations
Augmented Reality Critter Creation Tutorial

ELIZABETH A. GROSS, Library Science Assistant Professor

ULAN DAKEEV, Engineering Design Technology Assistant Professor

Sam Houston State University, Texas

A ugmented reality (AR) is ubiquitous, but how are its characters built? And how cool would it be for your program participants to be able to fashion such creations themselves? This program allows you to dabble in AR in a really easy, inexpensive way. We walk you through the entire process from concept to finished product. Watch your participants fly their own creation! Once participants go through this tutorial, they will also be able to use the software to create AR games and other activities. The computer OS is not important. The "how-to" included in this chapter has been done on a Windows machine, but Macs may be used as well. The reason we chose to use Google Android phones (as opposed to Apple iOS phones) is that the Apple Store requires you to register and pay fees in order to upload your creation. If you plan to do this, the opportunity is certainly available as a choice via the Unity software. However, in this section, we will demonstrate the less-expensive way to get your creations working.

Age Range	Type of Library Best Suited For	Cost Estimate
Tweens (ages 8–12) Young adults (ages 13–18) Adults	Public libraries School libraries Academic libraries	$0–$50

COST CONSIDERATIONS

Participants have the option to buy a creature. The one shown here is a free image. The sounds used are also free, but there are numerous other sound choices available that participants may choose to purchase.

OVERVIEW

A leader should be available to help participants work through the tutorial for this program. The tutorial offers step-by-step instructions with screen-shots to help learners follow along. The program will take approximately one hour to complete. The size of the group is limited to the technical skills of the audience. For younger participants, we suggest a ratio of four learners to one leader. For older participants, fewer leaders will be needed.

NECESSARY EQUIPMENT AND MATERIALS

- Computers (either laptops or desktops) that run either a Mac or Windows operation system
- Android phones
- Unity platform: https://unity3d.com/get-unity/download
- Vuforia Engine: https://developer.vuforia.com
- Dinosaur sound effects: https://www.zapsplat.com/sound-effect-category/dinosaurs/page/2

STEP-BY-STEP INSTRUCTIONS

Preparation

- Have a space where you can clearly hear and be heard. The main part of the library will not be appropriate for this project.
- The best setup will include some sort of visual projection so that partic-ipants can follow along with the leader(s).

Program Instructions: How to Install Unity and Vuforia

- A visual walk-through for the entire sequence of this tutorial can be found at https://myshsu-my.sharepoint.com/:w:/g/personal/ eag041_shsu_edu/EV7Zkm1B951EjPwWYCioR6oBhsSx8QUMQ79 Gn6YW4A59NQ?e=UHYXuQ.
- To install Unity, go to https://unity3d.com/get-unity/download, then click *Download Unity Hub*. Open the downloaded installer, accept the license and terms, click *Next*, click *Finish*, and then *Run Unity Hub*.
- Click *Manual Activation* to start the activation process.
- Click *Save License Request*, then click *Next*, and save the license file.
- Load the license file, then select the license file that you just saved.
- Sign into Unity using your account. If you have a Unity account already, you can sign in. If you do not have a Unity account, click *create one*.
- After signing in, click *New License Agreement*. Select *Unity Personal* and choose *I don't use Unity in a professional capacity*. Then click *Done* and exit out. After that, go back to Unity again (Unity should be on your desktop at this point).
- Once Unity Hub installation is complete, it is time to install the latest Unity software.
- Click *Installs,* select the latest version of Unity, and start the *Download/ Install* process.
- When installation is finished, click *Project*, then select *New* on the top right to start Unity.
- You will be welcomed by the Unity interface.
- Install the Vuforia package.

The AR application should work with your device's camera, which tracks the image target you provide to Unity. This image contains anchor points that Unity tracks. When these anchor points are detected, the application will load the 3D animated model that was provided previously. To develop the anchor points, you will need to generate a license code from Vuforia that will cross-reference the database and the image provided. Therefore, you will need to develop the license code and the image target database from Vuforia. *Note:* You can follow the next steps to generate a new account and download the Vuforia package for Unity. Your folder should contain the latest version of the Vuforia package for Unity (as of June 2020). Therefore, you should be able to import to Unity from the folder directly. To download the Vuforia package, follow these steps:

- Go to https://developer.vuforia.com and click *download*.
- Create a new account, then log in to Vuforia. Click *Downloads*, then click *Add Vuforia Engine to a Unity Project* or upgrade to the latest version.
- Click *Import* to add the Vuforia package to Unity.

AR Development Tutorial: Preparation for AR Application: Starting Unity, Importing Packages

- Start *Unity Hub*.
- Click *New*, then select your version (we have 2020.2.0a13 right now).
- Enter the name of your choice (in our case, we named it "Dragon_Animation;" for the sake of this example, we will continue to reference "Dragon_Animation"). Select the folder where you want to save the files, then click *Create*.
- You will be greeted by the Unity interface.

You will need to import a couple of packages to develop your AR application.

- Select *Assets*, then *Import New Package*, then navigate to the folder where you downloaded the latest Vuforia package (we labeled our folder: "9-1-7"). Next, select the Vuforia package, click *Open* and then *Import*. (*Note:* If the dialog box requests that you update to the current version, select *Update*.)

Next, import the database you downloaded from Vuforia.

- Select *Assets*, then *Import New Package*. Then navigate to the folder where you downloaded the database, select *Open*, and then *Import*.
- Import the file that you downloaded and saved. Select *Assets* and then *Import New Package*. Navigate to the folder where you downloaded the package, then select *Open* and click *Import*.

AR Application Development

Now that we have completed our housekeeping with Unity and the imported packages, it is time to start building our AR application.

- Right-click on the *Hierarchy* window (left portrait, gray area). Then select *Vuforia Engine* and then *AR Camera*.

- Click *Open Vuforia Engine Configuration* in *Inspector* (right, gray area with property tools). Next copy (Ctrl + C or Cmnd + C) the license key you saved in a Microsoft Word document. Next, use the paste command (Ctrl + V or Cmnd + V).
- Right-click on *Hierarchy*, then select *Vuforia Engine*, followed by *Image Target*, followed by *Inspector*. Under *Image Target Behavior Script*, Change *From Image* in the drop down menu to *From Database*. Next, change *Empty on Database* to the imported database (in our case, our database was labeled TestAR).
- In the *Hierarchy* window, select *ARCamera*, then *On Inspector*, followed by the *Transform* tab, and then *Position*. Change the Y position value to 1 (this will move the camera 1 unit in the Y direction). Next, select *Rotation*, then enter a *90 to X* value (this will rotate your camera facing the image target. At the bottom-right, you should see ARCamera showing the image target).
- From the *Project* panel (bottom gray panel), click *Assets* and then *Black Dragon*. Drag the *Dragon Model* to the work area. Next, click *Inspector*, then *Transform*, followed by *Position*. Enter *0, 0, 0 to X, Y, Z* values, respectively (this will align the dragon with the camera and image target. Click *Scale*. Enter *0.01, 0.01, 0.01 to X, Y, and Z*, respectively (this will scale the dragon to fit into the visible area).
- In the *Hierarchy* window, click on and drag the dragon model under the image target (simply select the dragon from *Hierarchy* and drop it on the *Image Target*).
- Click the *Play* button at the top of your screen. Show the image target to the camera (you should see your screen showing the dragon) to test the first AR application. Notice that the dragon is not animated. Next, we will configure the imported dragon file to animate.
- Click the *Play* button again to stop the test.

Animation of the Dragon

- Inside the *Dragon* folder in the *Project* panel, click *play* (triangle) next to the dragon model. Next, select *Armature Fly_New*.
- Press *Ctrl + D* to duplicate this animation. Click the triangle to collapse the model (notice, you have a duplicate of the *Armature Fly_New* animation outside the dragon model).

- Within the *Dragon* folder, right-click in the open gray area. Click *Create*, then *Animator Controller*.
- On the Project folder, select *Armature Fly_New Animation*. On *Inspector*, check *Loop Time*.
- Double-click the *New Animator Controller*, then drag and drop the *Armature Fly_New animation* to the *New Animator Controller* window.
- In the *Hierarchy* window, select *Dragon_Baked...* model under *Image Target*. In the *Project* folder, drag the *New Animation Controller* to *On Inspector*. Then select *Controller*.
- Click the *Play* button; the dragon should now be animated.

Congratulations. Your AR animated dragon is now working!

Adding Audio to the AR Project

First, you will need to import an audio file (dragon growl) to the project. To do so:

- Select *Assets* in the *Project* folder. Then create a new folder (right-click *create new folder*). Rename the file as "Audio." Then, double-click to enter the *Audio* folder.
- From the *Packages* folder (where you downloaded the files), click to drag and drop the "DinoGrowl" .mp3 file to the *Audio* folder in Unity.
- In the *Hierarchy* window, expand *Image Target* (click the triangle). Select the *Dragon_Baked_Actions...* file. On *Inspector*, click *Add Component*. In the search bar, Type "Audio Source." Select *Audio Source* (note that the audio source has surrounded the objects on the scene).
- On *Inspector* (make sure *Dragon_Baked_Actions* is selected), drag *DinoGrowl* from the *Audio* folder to *Audio Resources*. Then select *Audio-Clip*. (At this point, the audio source dinogrowl will play if you test the application by pressing the play button at the top of your screen.)

Publishing to Android Phone/Tablet

- Select *Player Settings*, then *Other Settings*, and then *Identification*. Type "com.silfgenson.dragonnew." Select *Minimum API Level*, then *Android 4.4 'KitKat'* and then *Close*.
- Click *Build* and watch Unity build your .apk file.

- You may transfer the newly built .apk file to your Android phone/tablet.
- Congratulations! Your AR application for Android devices is ready.

RECOMMENDED NEXT PROJECTS

Once you've successfully run this program in your library, you may also want to check out the following programs in this book:

- Chapter 8: "How to Create Augmented Reality Culture Expedition Experiences"
- Chapter 20: "Designing in Virtual Reality: Using Apps to Create and Make"
- Chapter 30: "Create an AR Game Based on Your Library's Catalog System"

The Experience of War
An Immersed Reality

SETH M. PORTER, Assistant Director of Digital Teaching,
Learning, and Scholarship and Head of Donald E. Stokes Library
for Public and International Affairs
Princeton University, New Jersey

n this project, I will discuss virtual reality and how this realistic and immersive simulation of a virtual environment, experienced through interactive software and hardware, can be applied to assist students in understanding the impact of warfare and the implementation of power. This project will illustrate how your participants can learn the emotional and physical toll of warfare without any risk of injury or harm. The Experience of War is an interactive application of active learning, policy discussion, and real-world implications of the decisions made. Your participants will truly understand the impact of military intervention on the different stakeholders involved without the fake glory perpetuated by the media. This will assist the participants in your program in making better decisions as future policymakers or just members of a polity by understanding the impact of violence.

Age Range	Type of Library Best Suited For	Cost Estimate
Adults This project is geared toward adult-age, upper-class college students.	Academic libraries	$150–$3,000

COST CONSIDERATIONS

This program has a high-cost variance, depending on the hardware used. The program could be applied successfully with Google Cardboard sets for $150, or a more immersive environment could be created using multiple Oculus Quest headsets, which would increase the cost.

OVERVIEW

In this program, your participants will have the opportunity to embed themselves in a dangerous environment to better understand war and its impact on the stakeholders involved. Participants are immersed in a virtual world while watching a 360 video on the *Fight for Fallujah* using head-mounted devices, ideally Oculus Quest headsets or Google Cardboard sets if needed. The video is followed by a Socratic dialogue.

The program should run between thirty minutes and one hour. This includes time for logistical setup, instructions, the VR experience, and the Socratic dialogue with your participants. Less than fifteen participants and two instructors are ideal for the program. This will help you minimize any logistical issues or confusion that can be caused by random movements. Extended reality as a pedagogical tool can assist your participants in truly understanding the content through embedded cognition, and this program will leave a lasting memory of the impact of war.

NECESSARY EQUIPMENT AND MATERIALS

- Head-mounted device
  - Oculus Quest
  - Google Cardboard sets
- Access to Wi-Fi
- CPU
  - Projector access
  - Speakers

Recommended but Optional Materials

- Designated space for movement

STEP-BY-STEP INSTRUCTIONS

Preparation

- Charge the Oculus Quest device(s)
- Instruct participants beforehand to bring their own smartphone if using Google Cardboard.
- Have participants download the Oculus Quest app or the YouTube app depending on the hardware used.
- Help familiarize participants with the operations of the hardware before the class begins.
- Turn off the sound on all the hardware.
- The instructor should have the video ready to stream live during the session with the audio on so the sound is consistently synched.

Program Instructions

Setup

- The instructor should show up early to the class and make sure all the preparation for the hardware is streamlined and ready to implement. If the hardware is not charged or your participants have not downloaded the correct applications, the logistical setup will be more time-consuming.
- The instructor should introduce the project and discuss the sensitive material that will be viewed and discussed.
- As your participants enter, have them go through the following steps:
  - Navigate to content: *The Fight for Falluja* 360 video at https://youtu .be/_AroUkmID6s, or have a bit.ly or QR code ready.
  - Have each participant load the video on their head-mounted device.
  - Instruct each participant to hit *Play* the moment you say "Go."
  - Assist the participants with any hardware problems.
- As your participants load the needed content, the instructor should load the same video on the CPU with the project app and audio on.
- When every participant is prepared, have your participants hit *Play* while you hit *Play* simultaneously. This will assure that the audio is completely synchronous across the program.

Experience

- The participants should watch the entire video and be able to move around if possible. They will be able to see children playing in the rubble, tanks rolling by, farmers going about their usual businesses, and enemy combatants in prison cells.
  - As instructor, be prepared for sudden movements from your participants. This may include dodging bullets or moving quickly from a loud explosion.
- Following the VR experience: the instructor should lead a Socratic dialogue with their participants. Example prompts could include the following:
  - How did seeing the impact of warfare make you reassess implementation policy?
  - How did the experience of being in a war make you feel?
  - How does military intervention impact the local populace?
- You should take this time to really let your participants express themselves. It can be an emotional dialogue, but you should shy away from controlling this output. This is the strength of the exercise, and you will be able to assist your participants in an experience they will not forget.

RECOMMENDED NEXT PROJECTS

If you enjoyed implementing this experience with your VR program and participants, you should look into adding additional emotional VR programs. This could include an introduction to immersive content in other disciplines, such as environmental sciences, where you could assist your participants in seeing the real damage of global warming.

The true strength of this type of initiative comes from the immersive opportunity your participants receive—they develop a sense of otherness and emotionally understand experiences they couldn't grasp without immersive technology.

Designing in Virtual Reality
Using Apps to Create and Make

HANNAH POPE, Emerging Technologies Librarian

Appalachian State University, North Carolina

U sing virtual reality to experience new things is great, but contributing to VR by creating your own content? Even better! This project describes how to engage your library patrons by having them create within the VR environment and learn about designing in 3D. You don't need to purchase expensive equipment or develop an academic lesson to create a program that promotes creativity in VR. In this program, we explore the various options available for all types of library personnel to help them select equipment, get the software, and then set goals for the program. Participants will use VR equipment to create something that will help them solve a problem or fulfill an assignment or just as a fun way to explore a new skill.

Age Range	Type of Library Best Suited For	Cost Estimate
Tweens (ages 8–12) Young adults (ages 13–18) Adults	Public libraries School libraries Academic libraries	$0–$800

COST CONSIDERATIONS

Costs are determined by the type of program you choose, the equipment you purchase or already possess, and what software you use.

OVERVIEW

This program includes guidance on how to come up with an objective for participants, then explores how to use the software to create an object, followed by the final step in the process: the presentation. The minimum time needed for participants to create a good product is an hour, though this program can be as short or long as you prefer; you can even spread it out across a few days. One to three staff members to oversee the program is sufficient because, after the initial training, it is up to the participants to create their objects. Some base-level tech support may be required to manage the VR equipment. Virtual projects can be created individually or in groups; so, it depends on the size of your space and the scale of your program.

NECESSARY EQUIPMENT AND MATERIALS

- One or more VR headsets (we recommend HTC Vive, Oculus Rift, or Oculus Quest)
- Gaming PC (if using a high-powered headset such as the HTC Vive or Oculus Rift)
- TV monitor (if using a high-powered headset or for group projects)
- Tilt Brush, Blocks, SculptrVR, CoSpaces, etc.—choose your preferred design software
- Space for setting up the appropriate equipment

Recommended but Optional Materials

- Prizes
- Paper and pencil for brainstorming and prototyping
- Food

STEP-BY-STEP INSTRUCTIONS

Preparation

- What do you want your audience to learn? If this project is for a grade, have the learning outcomes and rubric ready to go before the participants begin. When people are first introduced to VR design, it is a good idea to have a set list of things you are looking for. This applies to various events such as a Make-a-Thon or competition. Prepare the rules in advance and send them out to participants beforehand if possible. For example, if your program is a Make-a-Thon, the focus of the program could be to solve a problem related to conserving water using the VR program, Blocks. Each individual or team would be responsible for engineering something large or small in Blocks within a certain time frame. Make-a-Thons are typically run by teams over the course of a couple of days, but you could always modify this program to fit within a shorter time frame. Instead of trying to create something to conserve water, teams could create a practical part to fix a multipart device or design something as simple as a box that has a hidden panel. Libraries could also tailor these projects to go along with something related to current events. The possibilities are endless.
- Do you want this program to be competition-based, for a grade, or just for the sake of creating something? If this is for a competition or just as a means for participants to express creativity, think about where and how you can display the end results. Do you have digital signage that you can use to show off the participants' creative endeavors after the program? Many VR design programs can export videos of projects that could be made into a digital exhibit. If this is an academic project for a grade, decide how students will submit their projects. Some may choose to upload the projects as videos or screenshots, while some teachers actually take their students to where the VR system is located so that each person can present their finished product in the headset itself. Think about what you would like to happen after the project is over.
- Have you used the program? It is always a good idea to familiarize yourself with the software before you introduce it to your patrons. Besides helping with troubleshooting, taking this extra time to learn the ins and outs of the program will allow you to create a sample from start to finish,

therefore experiencing some of the challenges that the participants will later face. By providing an example (or two!) of what you expect as the finished product, you can more clearly articulate the desired result of the program.

Program Instructions

Setting Up Your Program

- Decide if your program is a competition, community event, graded lesson, or Make-a-Thon. Take into consideration the questions asked in the above section.
- Choose and purchase the design software you wish to use. It is important to decide on the software first because some applications work for certain VR headsets and others don't. For example, Tilt Brush only works on the more advanced headsets, typically at the level of an Oculus Quest and up.
- Purchase appropriate headsets if needed. Already have an HTC Vive? Great. In order to avoid buying additional headsets, consider making the event for groups or think about staggering the times between each individual session. Need to purchase equipment? Think about your budget, the type of equipment that works with your design software, how many pieces of equipment you need to purchase, and how you will be able to sustainably use that equipment after the initial event is over. *Note*: Some headsets require advanced graphics cards from gaming computers. These can get pricey; so, that may be a consideration regarding which direction you decide to go.
- Choose a site that makes sense for your anticipated number of participants. Make sure that there are plenty of power sources and enough room to allow participants to spread out and brainstorm without getting hurt. Some libraries have designated VR spaces, but these might not be large enough to accommodate all the people who attend your event. It is a good idea to make your VR setup somewhat mobile so that it can be in a larger part of the library if needed. Block off space and put up signs so that others in the library know that the event is happening and no one accidentally gets sideswiped by a VR controller.
- Advertise if you need to, or if this is for a course, let students know this is happening as far in advance as possible.

During the Program

- First, give all your participants either a link or a copy of the objectives of the project. For a competition or Make-a-Thon, outline the objective and rules. For a fun, low-stakes creative activity, make sure all the participants understand the parameters involved. For an assignment, participants should know the rubric.
- Introduce the technology. Many participants may not have had any experience with VR, much less designed something using this platform. Demonstrating how to use the equipment and software will reassure participants and hopefully cut down on troubleshooting later on.
- After the demonstration, let your participants know the exact time frame they have in which to deliver their projects (and remind them about the prizes if there are any). Depending on your program, split the teams into groups or let them start brainstorming and exploring with the VR software individually.
- Monitor the VR equipment once people begin to use it. There will undoubtedly be minor troubleshooting issues at the very least. We recommend having at least one backup headset in case of an emergency. If this is a one-shot experience, walk amongst the groups now and then to check on their progress. If this is a longer program, be available via e-mail for any residual questions. In the case of some projects, especially academic projects for a grade, once the project is explained, groups or individuals will often return to the library over the course of a few days to stagger the use of the equipment before the assignment is due. Many libraries use a booking system to help regulate such use.
- Document the progress of the participants on social media. This can be a fun way to connect with the people designing the pieces as well as with others who might want to see the final results.

Finishing Up the Program

- After the allotted time is over, gather the participants. Their finished projects usually turn out to be very inventive and creative, so it is worth having a "show and tell" session to wrap up the event. According to the format you chose, your participants' projects can be displayed via the VR equipment or through video(s) or pictures of the completed project.

- Let participants know if their work will be displayed in any way. It is always a good idea to also get permission from the participants before adding their designs to any type of exhibit.
- Award prizes if there are any.
- Elicit feedback through a survey or comment card.
- Share the successful event both in the library and on social media. This may drum up excitement for a similar, bigger event down the road.

RECOMMENDED NEXT PROJECTS

Now that you have completed this program, you can take it further by adding your own twist. If your project was set up as a contest, come up with concepts that tie into the greater mission of your institution or community. If sustainability is important, have participants create a project in VR that is a creative solution for solving a problem related to the environment. If you are teaching a course and integrating VR creation into the curriculum, come up with a project that pushes beyond the prototyping phase. Have participants create their designs in VR and then make a replica using another medium such as a 3D printer. Some programs, such as Blocks, are set up to export 3D files to achieve that goal. To push the program even further, participants can be tasked to create something by designing a unique VR environment using software such as Unity or Unreal Engine, where they can also incorporate more advanced coding and game development skills.

How to Create a VR Art Exhibition

CHRIS HOLTHE, Experiential Learning Librarian
Northern Arizona University's Cline Library

n this program, your participants will learn how to create unique works of three-dimensional art using the Tilt Brush virtual reality painting application. The resulting artwork can then be displayed by your library as part of a VR art exhibition that will serve to highlight the artistic accomplishments of your participants. While this chapter will chiefly emphasize the Tilt Brush app due to its ease of use and ubiquity across most VR platforms, the concepts and processes discussed can easily be adapted for use with any number of VR art apps. This program introduces your participants to the creative potential of VR while empowering them to express their creativity, imagination, and storytelling abilities in new and exciting ways.

Age Range	Type of Library Best Suited For	Cost Estimate
Young adults (ages 13–18) Adults	Public libraries School libraries Academic libraries	$420–$500-plus

COST CONSIDERATIONS

The overall cost of this program will depend largely on the model and quantity of VR headsets you choose to purchase. Many VR headsets that support six degrees of freedom (6DoF) start around $400, while app expenses will run you between $20 and $100 depending on the apps you choose to provide.

OVERVIEW

The VR Art Exhibition program will allow your participants to explore their artistic creativity in new and exciting ways through the medium of VR. In this program, participants will be given the opportunity to create immersive three-dimensional paintings using the Tilt Brush VR application. This artwork can then be compiled into a unique library display that will highlight individual creativity and demonstrate the artistic potential of VR. Not only is this program a great way to promote interactive VR experiences within your library, but it is also a simple and fun way to introduce first-time users to a virtual environment. Whether you work in a small community library or a large academic library, the structure of this program is extremely flexible and can be adapted to suit your needs. This program can be offered as a single limited-duration event or as an ongoing series, allowing you to compile the works of your participants over time.

The Tilt Brush app emphasized in this chapter allows participants to fill a virtual space with three-dimensional brush strokes using a variety of brush styles and colors. It is also extremely easy to use and is available on most VR platforms. While the instructions for this program are written for use with Tilt Brush, they can easily be adjusted for use with any of the optional VR art apps listed below. This program will also explore many unique ways of creating art exhibitions from the creative works of your participants, including exporting artwork as 2D and 3D images, GIFs, and videos for display, as well as turning VR sculptures into physical 3D printed models.

NECESSARY EQUIPMENT AND MATERIALS

- At least one VR headset capable of six degrees of freedom, such as the HTC Vive, Oculus Rift, Oculus Quest, Windows Mixed Reality, Valve Index, or PlayStation VR
- Please note that if you choose to use a tethered VR headset with a wired connection, you will also require a high-powered PC and viewing monitor.

- A dedicated play area for each headset measuring at least 5 × 5 square feet
- Sanitization materials such as Clorox wipes, lens cleaners, and disposable face masks
- Tilt Brush app (by Google)—$19.99
- Colorful masking tape or duct tape

Recommended but Optional Materials

- Kingspray Graffiti—$14.00—a VR graffiti simulator and street art app available on the HTC Vive, Oculus Rift, Oculus Quest, and Valve Index
- Gravity Sketch—$29.99—a VR sketching and 3D modeling app available on the HTC Vive, Oculus Rift, Oculus Quest, and Valve Index
- Google Blocks—Free—a VR sculpting and 3D modeling app available on the HTC Vive and Oculus Rift
- Oculus Medium—$29.99—a VR sculpting and 3D modeling app available on the Oculus Rift
- Oculus Quill—Free—a VR illustration and animation app available on the Oculus Rift
- LCD display screen(s)
- PLA 3D printer(s) and filament

STEP-BY-STEP INSTRUCTIONS
Preparation

- Set up and calibrate your VR headset(s). If you are using a tethered VR headset, you will also need to connect it to a PC and install the appropriate software for your device.
- Carefully mark out a separate play area for each headset using colorful tape. This play area should measure at least 5 × 5 square feet. For safety reasons, be sure to remove all furniture and other obstacles from the play area. If you are using a tethered VR headset, carefully organize and secure all the wires to ensure that your participants can move freely.
- Using the app store for your VR headset(s), download the Tilt Brush app by Google.
- Read through the list of optional VR art applications (above) and download any additional apps that you wish to provide to your program participants.

- Take some time to familiarize yourself with your selected app(s) so that you are prepared to provide training and direction to participants. This step is particularly important if you are using a stand-alone VR headset (such as the Oculus Quest) since you may need to verbally guide participants through the use of the app(s).
- Be sure to download and install any software updates before your program begins.

Program Instructions

To determine the best way to support this program based on the capabilities of your library, consider the following questions:

- Will you offer this program as a single event or an ongoing series? A single, limited-duration event allows you to attract more participants and to quickly accumulate a large body of VR content for your art exhibition. However, to fully support such an event, you may require multiple VR headsets and additional staff to train, supervise, and assist a large number of participants. If your library has a limited number of VR headsets or limited staffing, an ongoing VR art series can often provide the same level of engagement as a single event. In an ongoing series, headsets are circulated to individuals for short periods (ideally one to two hours) over the course of a few days or weeks. Participants can then work at their own pace and submit their artwork to staff upon completion.
- How long will your program last? The length of your program will largely be determined by the format you select and resources you have available. At minimum, each participant will need around fifteen to thirty minutes to acclimate to the Tilt Brush interface and begin the creation process. If possible, allow one to two hours per participant, which will result in more complex and polished artwork. If you choose the single-event format, you will need to calculate the amount of time you can afford each participant and be prepared to manage their time accordingly.
- How will you train your participants? Providing hands-on training on the use of Tilt Brush is ideal, particularly if you are offering this program as a single event. If you do not have the staffing resources to provide hands-on training to all your users, or if you plan to offer this program as an ongoing series, you may wish to provide training materials in the form of how-to videos or user guides.

- Are there legal conditions you must meet in order to display artwork? Be sure to check with your library administration as you may be required to follow strict artwork attribution requirements or collect signed release forms in order to legally display your participants' artwork.

The first component of your program will be to train your participants on the use of your selected VR app(s). The content of this training will vary depending on the model of VR headset and apps you select, but in general, you should cover:

- How to adjust and focus the VR headset
- How to hold and manipulate the hand controllers
- How to resize and move around the virtual environment (teleport)
- How to modify the tool palette to select between different tools and settings
- How to use the paintbrush, color selector, eraser, and the undo and redo tools
- How to use the camera tool to save images or videos of artwork

This training can be offered to each participant individually, to a large group simultaneously, or via training materials such as videos or how-to guides. If you are working with a large group, consider encouraging participants to assist one another.

While participants are working on their artwork, particularly if you offer a large-scale single event, staff should be on hand to answer questions or give instructions on how to properly manipulate the app interface.

Once participants have finished their artwork, instruct them on how to save their artwork for display (see instructions below). If required by your library, collect attribution information or signed release forms from each participant before they leave.

Sharing Artwork Online

Most VR art creation apps—including Tilt Brush, Kingspray Graffiti, Gravity Sketch, and Google Blocks—allow users to upload and share their artwork to online libraries. These libraries enable browsing, downloading, and 360-degree viewing of artwork using a computer, mobile device, or VR headset. To upload a sketch to Poly (Google's 3D library) using Tilt Brush:

- While in a Tilt Brush sketch, navigate to the *Tools* panel in the palette and select *Save Sketch*.
- Take a snapshot of the sketch to use as a thumbnail image.
- The sketch is now added to your account's Sketchbook. When using a tethered headset, the sketch file is also saved to your computer under *Documents*. Select *Tilt Brush* from the list of Documents and then *Sketches*.
- To upload the sketch to Poly (poly.google.com), navigate to the *Tools* panel in the palette and select *Upload*.

Displaying Artwork

To accommodate simple in-library art displays, many VR art creation apps—including Tilt Brush, Gravity Sketch, and Kingspray Graffiti—allow users to export 2D images or videos of their 3D creations. These images or videos can then be printed, displayed on screens, or uploaded to the web. To create an image or video of a sketch using Tilt Brush:

- While in a Tilt Brush sketch, navigate to the *Tools* panel in the palette and select *Cameras*.
- Using the joystick on the painting controller, choose between *snapshot (PNG)*, *auto GIF*, *5-second GIF*, or *video (MP4)*. Use the controller to record the image or video.
- When using a tethered headset, all images and videos will be saved to the *Documents* folder on the attached computer.
- These files can now be printed or uploaded to LCD display screens using a USB drive, PowerPoint slide show, or digital signage media player (such as BrightSign or Screenly).

3D Printing Sculptures

If you choose to offer VR sculpting apps in your program—such as Gravity Sketch, Google Blocks, or Oculus Medium—an exciting way to display your participants' sculptures is to translate their digital designs into physical 3D printed models. To 3D-print a VR sculpture:

- Browse the selected VR app's menu for exporting options. The exact location of the exporting options will differ between apps, but in general, look for exporting options for 3D model files (such as OBJ or STL file extensions).

- Upload the 3D model file to a computer and open it using the 3D printer's slicer program (such as MakerBot Print or Cura).
- Use the slicer program to resize or reorient the 3D model, as necessary.
- Use the slicer program to verify that the 3D model is solid. Examine the model for any areas that may not print correctly. Adjust infill and supports as necessary.
- Follow the instructions for your brand of 3D printer to finish printing the model.

RECOMMENDED NEXT PROJECTS

If your participants enjoyed this program, there are a number of other ways to design unique programming around VR creativity. You might consider framing your art exhibition as a competition based on a specific theme, idea, or work of literature. Or perhaps you might choose to encourage the design of more complex immersive artwork that incorporates music, audio, or animation in order to tell a story; this is a great way to spice up a story time! There are, of course, a wide array of other apps that bring creativity to life through VR. I highly recommend you explore apps such as Google Blocks (sculpting), Minecraft (construction), Jam Studio VR (music mixing), Mindshow (animation), or any of the dozens of VR storytelling apps. Most importantly, be creative and have fun!

Google's Tour Creator
Bringing Library and Classroom Tours to Life

BIANCA C. RIVERA, School Librarian

Ruth C. Kinney Elementary School, New York

E ager students often wonder what their new schools will look like. From the kindergartener anxious about their first classroom to the budding middle school basketball player excited about the school gymnasium to the senior in high school frantically awaiting a peek at the new eSports room, 360 photos can easily bring these spaces to life. Libraries can also take advantage of this technology to showcase their interiors and market programs. In this chapter, readers will learn how they can easily provide immersive 360 tours to their stakeholders using little more than a 360 camera and free/cheap software applications. There will also be recommendations for developing similar library programs for students and library patrons of all ages.

Age Range	Type of Library Best Suited For	Cost Estimate
Tweens (ages 8–12) Young adults (ages 13–18) Adults	Public libraries School libraries Academic libraries	A one-time cost of approximately $250–$500

FIGURE 22.1   Screenshot of scene creation in Google's Tour Creator

COST CONSIDERATIONS

The initial cost estimate may be off-putting; however, it is important to note it is for the one-time cost of hardware (for a 360 camera). After purchasing the camera, additional costs will be none to minimal, and the camera can be used for other projects. To get the full value of the camera, we recommend that a technology department (within the school district or library system) purchase the camera for interdepartmental use so it can be utilized by all school and library departments.

OVERVIEW

Once you learn how to use your 360 camera and its associated app or software, it should not take long to create a tour. In about a week, I completed this project alone and was able to learn everything I needed to know through online tutorials and just by experimenting. What took me the longest was learning how to use the 360 camera and how to take the best shots. There is a lot to consider when taking 360 shots for tours, which did not become apparent until I started looking at my first images. For tours intended for the public, it is important that the shots look professional, which means the photographer should not be in them. This cannot be accomplished unless the 360 camera is mounted on a mini tripod and the photo is taken remotely.

I ended up having to buy a mini tripod because they do not come with the cameras. I then utilized the app that comes with my 360 camera to take the photo so I would be out of the line of sight of the camera (for this project, I used an Insta360 ONE R camera and the Insta360 Camera control app).

After you learn how to use your 360 camera and take quality images, the rest is straightforward. I found Google's Tour Creator very intuitive and easy to use. Google, like YouTube, allows creators to host tours on their site and share tour links as unlisted or public.

Regarding the optional materials I list below, your users do not need VR viewers to enjoy your 360 tour! Such tours look great without the dedicated viewers because you are still getting the 360 view of the space. If your users or your library own viewers, that's an extra bonus that will make the tour more engaging. Likewise, you do not have to add audio to your tour, but if you'd like to make the tour more interactive, I recommend you use a microphone to record audio, which will give the program a more professional tone. Regarding image editing, you don't have to remove the image of the tripod and camera from your 360 photo, but it will add a touch of professionalism if you do.

NECESSARY EQUIPMENT AND MATERIALS

- 360 camera—note that Google's Tour Creator has a recommended list of 360 cameras on their help page (which vary in price). Cameras you can use for this project range in price from $250 to $500. In this project, I used an Insta360 ONE R Twin Edition. You should also have a microSD card for your camera.
- Camera app or software—note that for this project, I used the Insta360 Camera control app. A different 360 camera will most likely have its own associated camera control apps (often free).
- Mini tripod—there are specially built smaller tripods meant for 360 cameras; I recommend using one with a small footprint (about $12).
- Google's Tour Creator (free) and the latest Chrome browser

Recommended but Optional Materials

- Image editing app or software to remove the image of the tripod and camera—I used the TouchRetouch app ($1.99).
- Microphone for recording audio narration in Tour Creator (about $40)
- Google Cardboard or any other VR viewer that uses a smartphone (about $15)

STEP-BY-STEP INSTRUCTIONS

Preparation

- First and foremost, consider your space. Remember: Your goal is to create a professional-looking tour, and first impressions count. You want your "visitors" to feel like they are there, experiencing the space firsthand. Put away clutter, throw away trash, and decide beforehand if you want people in your photos (including yourself). Ideally, you and your camera should not appear in the images. Find a way to take the photos remotely, and use an image editing app to remove the camera and tripod from the photo.
- Will your viewers look at your tour on a computer or mobile device, or do you want users to have the full VR experience using dedicated software? These types of tours look great on computers and mobile devices; so, it's okay if you do not have dedicated viewing devices. Do not let that detract you from completing this project! However, if you want to purchase such equipment, Google Cardboard viewers are more than adequate and are only $15 each.
- Can your users read (consider young children or users who do not read English)? If they do not, and you have added text narration, consider adding audio narration to your Google Tour. If users are not native English language speakers, consider adding text and narration in another language.
- If you are new to 360 cameras, take your time getting acquainted with them. This is an extremely different experience from using a regular camera or the camera on your phone. Watch YouTube tutorials, and most importantly, get out there and practice taking test shots of your space.

- Look at sample tours on Google's Tour Creator website. See how others have designed their tours and how they used the *Points of Interest* and *Image Overlays* tools most effectively.

Program Instructions

- After preparing your space, use your 360 camera to take multiple still photos of the room. Although 360 cameras can capture an entire room, I recommend you take several shots of various areas within your room to capture all the hidden spots (i.e., different areas of the print collection, reading nooks, teaching area, circulation desk, catalog computers, Makerspace, tech corner, and so forth). Keep in mind, tours are intended for future students, current students, and parents/guardians; so, include photos of areas that viewers need to be aware of.
- Using your camera's native app or software, review your shots, and convert them to one of Google's Tour Creator's acceptable file types (.jpeg, .jpg, .png). It is highly recommended that you back up your original 360 files. If you delete them from your microSD card, it will be virtually impossible to get them back. Save the original files to the cloud or your PC. You can always convert and/or edit the JPGs, but once the original files are deleted from a portable drive, they're gone!
- Decide what image editing software or app you will use to remove the tripod and camera from your images (if you decide to do so). For example, if you use the recommended TouchRetouch app, you will need to put your JPG files in the cloud and open them using the TouchRetouch app. After removing the tripod and camera, you need to resave the image files and send them back to the cloud where you can access them for the tour.
- If you have multiple Google accounts, decide which one you want to use to host your tour. Sign into Google with that account, visit Google's Tour Creator, and click *New Tour*.
- Select a cover photo for your tour (*note*: this will display as a standard shot, not a 360 image). Title your tour and provide a sufficient description of it for your viewers (up to fifty words). You can assign your tour a category, but notably, education is not one of the category options (I ended up selecting *Places & Scenes*). Click *Create*.
- Click *Add Scene* to start adding scenes (i.e., your edited 360 photos) to your tour. Ideally, you will have different scenes for each of the main

areas of your space that you want visitors to explore. There is an option to use *Street View* for your scene, but if using your own images, you can click *Upload*. Then, upload the 360 photo that showcases your scene and click *Add Scene*.

- Once you have created a scene, take some time to think about what you want to share with your viewers. You can provide a written description of the scene (up to five hundred words), and if you so choose, record narration reading the description (must be in a .mp3 file format). You can also upload ambient audio if you'd like to mimic the sound of the space, but make sure to use royalty-free files (you can search for free children's classroom sound files—that will make your tour sound very authentic!). Note that adding ambient audio and scene narration are two different options (they have two different selection symbols). Make sure to give yourself credit for your photos (under *Credits*).
- Don't forget to add points of interest to your photos when necessary. Using this feature will superimpose a letter *i* in a circle on your photo. Your users can click on this to get detailed information (up to fifty words) about an area of your photo. You can add a text description for the point of interest as well as an image overlay and narration.
- Whenever you upload a 360 photo, you will see a small circle symbol and the words *Set starting view*. Always click on that and scroll to the area you want your users to see first.
- It is important to note that you need to do your own spellcheck as Tour Creator does not highlight misspelled words. Either enable spellchecking within your browser or copy and paste your text into a Google Doc or Microsoft Word document to do a spellcheck.
- When your tour is complete, click the blue *Publish* button. This will publish your tour to Google's Poly (a website created by Google that hosts 3D assets). Your tour can be unlisted or public, and you will be provided a link for sharing.
- One great feature of this program is that you can always go back to your tour and edit anything (images, text, audio, etc.). So, if you find an error after your tour is published or you need to update images based on physical changes in your space, you can do so and then republish your tour.
- You can also embed a tour on a website. Visit your tour on the Poly website, click *Share* and then *Embed*. You can then copy and paste the embed code into your website.

- If you ever need to delete a tour, do so from Tour Creator and the Poly website. Make sure you are signed into the Google account you used to create the tour.
- You (and your users) can also view your tour in the Google Expeditions app. Make sure you are signed into Google with the same account you created your Google Tour in. Visit the Expeditions app on your phone, click *Library* and then *My Tours* to download and view your tour!

RECOMMENDED NEXT PROJECTS

After you complete your virtual tour, try turning this into a library program and let students or patrons in on the fun! Teach others how they can create a virtual tour of their own. If you work at a school, teach students and classroom teachers how to create virtual tours of their classrooms. For example, a grade school student or teacher could create a tour showing important classroom routines and procedures and highlighting important areas of the classroom. If you work at a public library, show public services departments how they can showcase public areas and explain patron procedures.

After you have completed this program, see chapter 23: "Creating Immersive VR Library Tours with CoSpaces Edu" for another way to incorporate VR tours into your programming.

A link to my final Google Tour can be found by searching for "Ruth C. Kinney Elementary Library" on Google's Poly website or by visiting this link: https://poly.google.com/view/fHUM7bDMjFR. For Google Tour Creator help, visit Google's Tour Creator's official help page: https://support.google.com/tourcreator.

Creating Immersive VR Library Tours with CoSpaces Edu

BIANCA C. RIVERA, School Librarian

Ruth C. Kinney Elementary School, New York

Teachers wanting to expose their students to the gamut of currently in-demand technical skills, such as 3D modeling, 360 images, and coding, as well as the traditional skills of writing and collaboration, would do well to adopt CoSpaces Edu into their curriculum. CoSpaces Edu allows users to build 3D experiences, animate them with code, and engage with them in virtual reality. Leveraging the popularity of Project-Based Learning, teachers can assign projects that allow students to create immersive worlds to showcase their learning.

In this chapter, readers will learn how they can easily create immersive 360 tours of their spaces incorporating 3D objects to enhance the experience for users. Aspects of this project are similar to creating tours in Google's Tour Creator (as seen in chapter 22 of this book), yet the uniqueness of the product allows CoSpaces Edu to take the virtual experience to the next level. Readers will be referred to chapter 22: "Google's Tour Creator: Bringing Library and Classroom Tours to Life" during this article.

Age Range	Type of Library Best Suited For	Cost Estimate
Tweens (ages 8–12) Young adults (ages 13–18) Adults	Public libraries School libraries Academic libraries	A one-time cost of approximately $250–$500

COST CONSIDERATIONS

The cost of this project is based on a one-time cost of hardware (for a dedicated 360 camera). Although there are cell phones that can take 360-degree panoramas, I do not recommend this method as it is difficult to get the stitching correct (the process of merging multiple images into one to make them appear seamless). Aside from purchasing the camera (I used an Insta360 ONE R), the only other cost depends on whether you license a CoSpaces Edu Pro plan or stick with the Basic plan, which is free. For the purposes of this project, I was able to use the free plan. Though limited compared to the licensed plan, it did everything I needed to create a classroom tour.

OVERVIEW

Having reviewed the methods outlined for taking 360 shots in chapter 22, I recommend readers refer to that chapter for tips on taking 360 photos.

Regarding the optional materials listed below: Your users do not need VR viewers to enjoy your 360 tour built with CoSpaces Edu. These tours look great even without the dedicated viewers because you are still getting a panoramic view of the space. However, tours built with CoSpaces and paired

FIGURE 23.1   Image of coding a scene in CoSpaces Edu

with 3D models are especially engaging; so, if you can view the tour with 3D viewers, you'll be in for a treat. You also do not have to add audio to your tour, but if you'd like to make the experience more interactive, I recommend using a dedicated microphone to record audio for more professional sound quality. Regarding image editing, you don't have to remove the image of the tripod and camera from your 360 photo, but doing so will add a touch of professionalism to the experience.

NECESSARY EQUIPMENT AND MATERIALS

- 360 camera—CoSpaces Edu does not offer a recommended list of 360 cameras. An online search of the latest reviews on these types of cameras will help you narrow down your selections. Quality cameras range in price from $250 to $500. I used an Insta360 ONE R and was happy with it, largely due to the camera control app and image software (both free) that come with it.
- Mini tripod—there are smaller tripods specifically meant for 360 cameras. Get one with a small footprint (approximate price: $12).
- CoSpaces Edu—the Basic plan is free; Pro plans start at $74.99 (at the time of this writing). CoSpaces Edu is available on all platforms: browser-based for PCs and as an app for Chromebooks and mobile devices.

Recommended but Optional Materials

- Image editing app or software to remove the image of tripod and camera—I used the TouchRetouch app ($1.99)
- Microphone for recording audio narration (approximately $40)
- Google Cardboard or any other VR viewer that uses a smartphone (approximately $15)

STEP-BY-STEP INSTRUCTIONS
Preparation

- Look at sample tours on the CoSpaces Edu Gallery to get ideas for your own tour. Search for "tour" in the search box on the *Gallery* page.

- Browse through the *Creation Toolbox* in CoSpaces Edu to see what 3D models are available. Consider which characters or other 3D objects will go best with your theme. Think about 3D object placement, visibility, and whether any characters will be "speaking." Will you use 3D signs to convey information to your viewers? Where will they be placed? Will you be adding audio narration? If so, will you be narrating what your characters are "saying" or something else?
- If you are using the free version of CoSpaces Edu, keep in mind that you will be limited to using up to ten scenes for your tour. Therefore, you should take ten 360 shots of your space that highlight the most important areas of your library or space.
- See chapter 22 information about image files, but don't forget to back up your original 360 files after converting them to .jpg files.
- Keep in mind that this is a tour; you want it to look professional. See chapter 22 for additional tips. Remember: Your space should be clean and free of clutter. Most importantly, use a mini tripod with your 360 camera so you can remotely take a photo and keep yourself out of the image. Use an image editing app to remove the tripod and camera (and anything else you do not want included) from the images.
- CoSpaces Edu does allow for the inclusion of text in tour scenes; however, large text boxes can distract from images. If you have a lot of information to share, you may want to consider taking the time to record audio.
- It is important to note that you need to perform your own spellcheck as CoSpaces Edu does not highlight misspelled words. You should either enable spellchecking within your browser or copy and paste your text into a Google Doc or Microsoft Word document to run a spellcheck before adding it to the tour.
- If you are new to block coding, watch some CoSpaces Edu block coding video tutorials on YouTube. The block coding used to create my tour is very basic and easy to duplicate. However, if you want to get really interactive, you will need to take the time to learn how to block code. CoSpaces Edu uses Blockly; so, their block coding is similar to Scratch's code system.

Program Instructions

- After you have signed up for CoSpaces Edu, log in and look for CoSpaces on the left sidebar (under *Gallery* and *Classes*) and then click + *Create CoSpace.*

- You will then be prompted to choose a scene. Since you are creating a tour using your own 360 photos, click *360 Image* and then *Empty Scene.* You should then see a blue, starry background. On the bottom left corner of the screen, click *Environment.* Next, click *Edit.* You will be prompted to select a 360 photo. Select the one that will be used for your opening scene and then click *Open.*

- Now that you have your first scene, you need to add 3D objects to it. On the bottom of the screen is a *Library* tab. Click that and decide which 3D objects you want to add to your scene. I used the *Characters* and *Building 3D objects* for my tour.

- Once you drag and position the 3D objects to the location where you want them on the scene, you can edit or program them. In my tour, three-dimensional signs were used to explain what viewers were looking at in the scene. You can double-click on the signs to edit their text or change their font size.

- The characters can be programmed to do certain things. Once you drag a character out from the *Library*, double-click on them and then click *Code.* Make them programmable by turning on *Use in CoBlocks.* Once you do that, click *Code* (on the top-right of the screen) and then click *CoBlocks.* Decide what you want to happen when the viewer clicks on the character.

- For the purposes of a tour, it's important to add code blocks that will enable characters to speak. I used *Event* blocks that expressed: *When a Character is Clicked.* I used *Action* blocks that expressed: *Character to say "Message,"* and *Set Animation of Character to Animation Type.* I programmed my characters similarly throughout my ten scenes. You can right-click code blocks to copy and paste them from one scene to another. I then simply edited which character was speaking or moving.

- If you are adding audio, you can record your audio directly in CoSpaces or upload the .mp3 or .wav file. Make sure to do so for each individual scene of the tour. Keep in mind that you do not have to add narration; you can add background sounds instead to make your tour more realistic. Try searching Google for "free classroom sound effects" and limit your search to .mp3 or .wav file types.

- When you are done with your first scene, make sure to set your starting view of your image by panning to exactly what you want your viewers to see first. However your image is displayed is what your viewers will see first.
- After you are done with your first scene, look on the left side of the screen and click on the sidebar to see your completed scenes. Click + *New Scene* to create the next scene for your tour. Ideally, you will have different scenes for each of the main areas of your space that you want visitors to explore.
- You will start the process over again for your next scene. Just as before, you will need to upload the next 360 image for your tour. You will need to add 3D objects (characters and a sign) to your scene. You will also need to program your character to speak or move and add audio effects. Do this for the remaining scenes of your tour.
- When you are done creating your tour, click *Share* (on the top-right of the screen). Decide how you want to share your tour (either unlisted or in the *Gallery*). From there, you can add your *Sharing details*. Give your tour a descriptive name and provide a sufficient description for your viewers. Decide if you want to allow others to make a copy of your CoSpace. You can share your CoSpace in several ways. You can simply share the link, get an embed code to embed a CoSpace on a website, or post it on social media sites.
- A great feature of this software is that you can always go back to your tour and edit anything (images, text, audio, etc.); so, if you find an error after your tour is published, or you need to update images based on physical changes in your space, you can do so and then click *Share* and *Update* to share the updated version.
- If you ever need to archive or permanently delete your CoSpace, sign in, go to your CoSpace, click on the three dots next to your space, and click *Archive* or *Delete Forever*.
- As mentioned before, CoSpaces look great on a PC browser, but they look *amazing* in a dedicated 3D viewer. If you view the finished tour on a mobile device via the CoSpaces Edu app, you can view it in *Play*, *Gyro*, or VR mode. *Play* mode allows you to view the tour as you would on a PC. *Gyro* mode lets you move your device to look around your CoSpace through the screen. VR mode allows you to view your tour through a headset, and that is the ultimate experience!

RECOMMENDED NEXT PROJECTS

After you complete your virtual tour, try turning it into a library program and let students or patrons in on the fun! Show classroom teachers how to create a tour demonstrating classroom routines and procedures. Collaborate with a classroom teacher on a Project-Based Learning assignment such as digital storytelling or exhibition presentations. CoSpaces Edu has several high-quality lesson plans loaded onto their website that are free to use and adapt. For an alternative to creating virtual tours using CoSpaces Edu, see chapter 22: "Google's Tour Creator: Bringing Library and Classroom Tours to Life" for another way to incorporate virtual tours into your programming.

A link to my final CoSpaces Edu Library Tour is available online. I enabled *Remixing* so readers could copy over my tour and code. The tour can be found by visiting this link: https://edu.cospaces.io/VGD-CJY.

- CoSpaces Edu lesson plan on creating classroom tours: https://cospaces .io/edu/code-the-classroom-lesson-plan.pdf
- CoSpaces Edu lesson plan on digital storytelling: https://cospaces.io/ edu/storytelling-lesson-plan.pdf
- The Official CoBlocks Coding Reference Guide: https://cospaces.io/edu/ CoBlocks-Reference-Guide.pdf?_ga=2.84245593.1516716200.1598572766 -1696918686.1598202622

Creating VR Exhibits Based on Digital Collections

SCOTT FRALIN, Exhibits Program Manager and Learning Environments Librarian

WEN NIE NG, Digital Collections Librarian

Virginia Polytechnic Institute and State University

U sing the free online software, Artsteps, you will be able to easily create a virtual exhibit that visitors can explore through an internet browser on a computer or on their smartphone using the Artsteps app. You can build this exhibit using any existing digital collections with various formats, including images, audio, video, and 3D models. Visitors to the virtual exhibit will have the opportunity to explore your digital content in a safe manner which is most effective when creating a physical exhibit or display for them to explore in person is not possible. This chapter is for people or organizations who have digital collections ready and an interest in creating an interactive virtual exhibit. We will describe how to create an engaging experience for your participants with practical tips on efficient production of the exhibit using Artsteps.

Age Range	Type of Library Best Suited For	Cost Estimate
Kids (ages 3–7) Tweens (ages 8–12) Young adults (ages 13–18) Adults	Public libraries School libraries Academic libraries	$0–$50

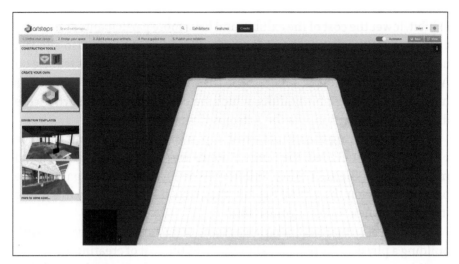

FIGURE 24.1   Building a virtual exhibit using the Artsteps online software

COST CONSIDERATIONS

While you do not have to pay anything to use Artsteps, there are some potential costs if you want to embed the exhibit on a web page rather than link to
it from the Artsteps website or host an in-person event. To build a website
around the Artsteps virtual exhibit, you might need to purchase web hosting
if you cannot use your library website or if you do not have your own site.
The advantage of having a web page dedicated to the virtual exhibit is that
you can include extra information about the exhibit and potentially link to
other content you want participants to see.

If you want to have an in-person event where participants can view the
virtual exhibit, consider investing in basic VR headsets that smartphones
fit into so participants can explore it in VR. The cost of these headsets
begins at $10 for the most basic gear (https://arvr.google.com/cardboard/
get-cardboard).

OVERVIEW

This project was originally planned as an in-person exhibit, but in response
to the COVID-19 pandemic, we chose to make it virtual. This change to virtual offered several benefits: we were able to include a lot more items in the

exhibit, lower the cost of the exhibit, and have more participants attend and view the exhibit whenever and from wherever they chose. It also allowed us to more accurately track participants through the view count feature on Artsteps, through Google Analytics on the web page where the exhibit was hosted, and through bit.ly links, which we used to track users who were drawn to our collections via the Artsteps virtual exhibit.

While exploring the virtual exhibit, participants learn about the type of collection(s) included, the range of items we collected, the purpose and mission of our digital library, and how to navigate a virtual space. Once participants enter the virtual exhibit, they have the opportunity to explore it on their own or follow a guided tour.

Creating a virtual exhibit removes some of the limitations involved with building a physical, in-person exhibit such as the cost of creating a physical exhibit, space limitations, space scheduling, and the limited availability of patrons to see it in person. We are aware of the limitations of a virtual exhibit as well, such as internet access, device or computer ownership, and the accessibility limitations of an exhibit on Artsteps. We solved the problem of accessibility within the Artsteps app by creating a separate, accessible exhibit using Omeka, which allowed patrons to view the exhibits online, though without the virtual experience. Creating a virtual exhibit like this requires you to make some sacrifices, but we felt that the end result of being able to share our collections in a safe way for exhibit visitors was worth it.

Communication and transparent operation were major factors in making the exhibit a success. Our collection managers, student workers, and collection partners were well-informed before creation of the exhibit began. After the exhibit prototype was done, a demo video hosted on YouTube was sent to collaborators for feedback. Frequent communication and appropriate credits inspired our team members to take the initiative and promote the virtual exhibit on their social media pages or institute website. The exhibit was further promoted by the crew on their personal social media accounts.

NECESSARY EQUIPMENT AND MATERIALS
Software

- Artsteps
- Collaboration tools (Google Docs, Google Sheets, YouTube)

Hardware

- Computer with internet access

Materials

- Image-based digital objects ready for exhibit

Recommended but Optional Materials

Software

- Video and audio editing software for feedback from partners; e.g., Adobe Premiere, iMovie
- Server hosting website/web hosting service
- Website building or content management software; e.g., WordPress, Omeka
- Short link generator; e.g., Bit.ly
- Web analytics service; e.g., Google Analytics

Hardware

- Building bricks such as LEGOs for visualizing your floor-plan blueprint
- Writing instruments for drawing floor-plan blueprints

STEP-BY-STEP INSTRUCTIONS

Artsteps

Preparation

- Prepare a list of interesting items (images, audio, video, curatorial writings, 3D objects) for your exhibit.
- Liaise with collection owners/partners (if any) for items to decide on their appropriateness for the exhibit.
- Research for more exhibit context and liaise with collection owners to add the necessary information to any items missing metadata so audiences know what they are looking at.

- Create an Artsteps account.
- Familiarize yourself with the Artsteps software.

Program Instructions

Building an exhibit on Artsteps involves five steps. Use the Artsteps manual concurrently with our guidelines. For details of each of the steps/functions (*Build & Delete Walls; Add & Remove Doors, Colors and Textures on Surfaces; Place Artifacts, Delete Artifacts, Positioning Artifacts; Place Guide Points; Save your Progress*) involved with building your exhibition, visit https://www .artsteps.com/categories/help.

- On the Artsteps interface, click *Create* to start creating your virtual exhibition.
- Define the space appropriate for your exhibit. There will be two exhibition templates and one *Create your own space* option available.
- If you choose *Create your own space*, draft a floor-plan blueprint for your virtual exhibition to cater to different collection sizes and start with defining the space by *Building walls* and then *Designing your space*. Otherwise, go to the next step.
- List all of the artifacts* you wish to display in the exhibit on an inventory list with the artifacts' functionality for ease of editing; i.e., for each of the text artifacts, list out the artifacts and their properties, such as *title/Text*, *Alignment*, *Interactive*, and *Description*. This will save a lot of time at the later phase of the process during QC and help you in deciding whether to turn on or off the interactive feature for the artifacts.
- Upload your artifacts (images, audio, videos, objects, text).
  - For our project, we offer books and 3D objects that we want our participants to interact with. We worked around the software by embedding the objects' distinct URL into the artifacts' *Description* to retain the interactive functionality.
    » *3D objects*: We used the Poly API asset library from Artsteps for a representative 3D object for our 3D objects. Participants will have to click on the 3D objects in the virtual exhibit and

---

*Items for the exhibit are defined as artifacts in Artsteps, which includes images, videos, objects, and text.

copy-paste the unique link hosted by Sketchfab, where they can interact with the 3D objects. Gamification of the exhibit is achieved by integrating 3D specimens into the nature scene of the exhibit to engage participants. Participants will have to explore to find the hidden 3D objects such as bug specimens.

» *Books:* We embedded the books' distinct URL into the artifacts' *Description* to redirect participants to our Omeka page, where participants can use a two-page view function just as one would read a book, with two pages aligned next to each other. Make sure the *Interactive* button is turned on so participants can copy and paste the URL from the pop-up modal window when they interact with the artifacts.

– In this project, we created bit.ly links for each of the URLs in the virtual exhibit on top of the embedded Google Analytics (GA) on our library exhibit web page. The rationale for this is that GA is challenging to track on iframe.

- Place your artifacts on the defined space.
- Switch to first-person view in the virtual space and walk around in the exhibit space. Check for smooth traffic flow, then evaluate the image size, image color tone, text font size, wall color, atmosphere, and environment of the virtual exhibit; i.e., make sure the lighting reflected on the images matches the setting of the image in the virtual exhibit.
- Next, place guide points if you want to create a guided tour. (This feature is not used in this exhibit.)
- Before publishing your exhibit, edit the following: *Title, Description,* and *Categories,* and then upload the audio file you have chosen to play throughout the exhibition.
- Click the *Show in Artsteps* option under *Publishing Settings* to publish your exhibit!

Accessible Exhibit

Preparation

Artsteps doesn't include accessible features within the software. To comply with ADA Section 508, we built another exhibit page within Omeka (a content management software) as an accessible alternative to the virtual exhibit.

Our temporary digital library was built on top of Omeka; so, we could use our assets database to more easily build our exhibit.

Program Instructions

Choose the items from the inventory list created from the virtual exhibit to be included on the Omeka exhibit page. Detailed instructions can be found at https://omeka.org/classic/docs/Plugins/ExhibitBuilder.

RECOMMENDED NEXT PROJECTS

Once you have completed your virtual exhibit using Artsteps, there are many things you can do to enhance or expand on the experience.

- Design a scavenger hunt for participants to complete while in the virtual exhibit. If the exhibit is for a class or school, the scavenger hunt could serve as a quiz or a bonus point assignment.
- If it is safe to do so, you could host an in-person event with some computers and simple smartphone-compatible VR headsets to teach patrons how to use Artsteps as well as invite them to view your digital collections.
- Use Artsteps to build simple games participants can play. You can create a maze-like room for them to navigate and hide clues on the walls, and so forth. Let your imagination go wild!
- Themed virtual exhibits in Artsteps can be a fun way to enhance existing holiday programming. For example, a Halloween virtual exhibit would be a very fun addition to a Halloween event.
- If you are teaching with Artsteps, consider having students go through the exhibit before class and then hold a discussion about it during class time. This can help support a flipped-classroom approach.
- Create a virtual version of an existing physical exhibit to expand the number of patrons who can access it.

If you want to do something a little more advanced, consider these ideas:

- Create your own 3D objects to use in Artsteps using free online software such as Tinkercad, 3D Splash, or SculptGL.

- Create an empty virtual sculpture garden and invite participants to create their own 3D objects to fill it! This would be a great way to teach people about 3D modeling and introduce some free tools that are available to beginners.
- If you want to try some software options that are more advanced than Artsteps, explore Unity and Mozilla Hubs.

When it comes to what you can do with Artsteps and its virtual exhibit capabilities, let your imagination go wild and don't eliminate any possibilities. Our list is just a start. We're confident that you will have just as many unique ideas as we did—probably even more!

ArtEdge

A Multidisciplinary Art and Tech VR Experience for School Children

KRISTI WYATT, Emerging Technologies Librarian

JOHN GRIME, Emerging Technologies Developer

University of Oklahoma

A rtEdge is an annual, themed, three-part program designed to teach twenty-first-century skills through collaborative and engaging work via the synthesis of art and technology. The program is intended to bring together various stakeholders in the library/museum community to collaborate in presenting the process and results of academic research to children in an engaging, interactive way. Students will first engage with a work of art and learn about Close Looking, then proceed to a "tech" component to view the artwork in virtual reality, which provides a safe means of manipulating the object. Finally, students will meet with a third-party collaborator appropriate to the theme chosen for the program that year. After experiencing the work in both physical and digital form, the students will work with the collaborator and create a group project to realize a physical expression of what they saw that day. ArtEdge gives students a well-rounded view of how technology can inform research and how the results of this research can be presented in interesting/interactive ways.

Age Range	Type of Library Best Suited For	Cost Estimate
Tweens (ages 8–12) Young adults (ages 13–18)	Public libraries School libraries Academic libraries	$400–$2,500 (depending on local expertise)

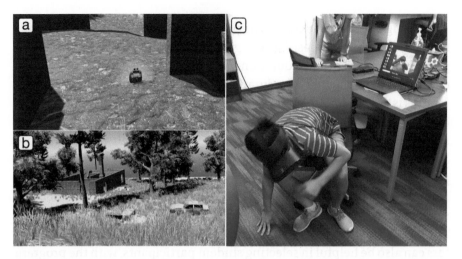

FIGURE 25.1 (A) Screenshot of the focal object inside the VR experience; (B) Screenshot of the building enclosing the object; (C) Student exploring the VR experience.

COST CONSIDERATIONS

Cost is dependent on the number of VR headsets and computers and the amount of art/craft supplies available/needed. If no local software development is allowed or possible, additional funds may be required for the adaptation/development of your VR software. However, free examples and tutorials for developing simple VR experiences using platforms such as Unity are quite common; it is, therefore, possible to create such experiences in-house, even in the absence of traditional software development experience.

OVERVIEW

The ArtEdge program involves a variety of stakeholders, and the preparation should start at least six months prior to the program start date once stakeholders are identified. This will allow for the selection of the artwork/artifact and execution of the narrative behind it, selection of the third-party collaborator, any 3D scanning that might be needed to generate digital content, and development of the scene in VR.

ArtEdge works best when participants are split into several small groups meeting at different times; e.g., five groups of ten students with each group participating once over the duration of the program. As group visits depend on stakeholder availability, the duration of the program can vary; two to three months is a good amount of time for five separate group visits. The number of headsets available is helpful when determining an appropriate group size. In some instances, if 3D scanning is involved (such as the Structure Sensor iPad scanner), students can split tech participation by working in pairs with one student in VR while the other learns how to make a quick 3D scan. When looking for participants, it is helpful to reach out to neighboring school districts as there might be a gap in programming, and an event such as ArtEdge might be just what they need. School teachers and administrators can also be helpful in selecting student participants, with the program treated like a field trip for the participants. Along with any teachers/adult supervisors available to oversee the program, we recommend that at least two to three personnel be present to help facilitate each visit.

NECESSARY EQUIPMENT AND MATERIALS

- VR headsets (e.g., Oculus or HTC Vive headsets)
- Computers with graphics cards suitable for use with the specific VR hardware
- Unity software development platform (free download)
- Building supplies (glue, construction paper, cardboard, scissors, tape, paint, beads, and so forth)
- A room or dedicated space containing sufficient tables and chairs
- VR presentation software (e.g., OVAL from the University of Oklahoma Libraries or a similar product)
- Blender (free modeling software)

Recommended but Optional Materials

- Structure Sensor iPad scanner (to simplify the creation of virtual objects to place in the VR scene)

STEP-BY-STEP INSTRUCTIONS

Preparation

- Find a third-party collaborator with an interest in high-tech approaches in their field of work/expertise, such as an archeologist, interior designer, and so forth.
- With the help of your collaborator(s), select your artwork (painting, sculpture, historical building, etc.). If 3D models of the artwork are available, this will offer a distinct advantage as such models will reduce the work required to create the experience.
- Choose a theme with the artwork in mind.
- Define the narrative: How is the selected third-party collaborator implementing tech into their own research? Does it relate to a piece in the museum's collection?
- Digital content development process:
  - Determine what is required to make the artwork multimodal and what is required to represent the environment in which the artwork "lives." The artwork itself should be the primary focus; so, most effort should be dedicated to creating a good-quality facsimile (potentially using techniques such as 3D scanning).
  - If in-house generation of the representation is not possible, internet searches and websites, such as Sketchfab, can sometimes provide a suitable substitute.
  - If the focus of the experience is architectural (specific buildings or rooms in a building), simply reproducing the appropriate structure may be sufficient. If additional surrounding environment is required as context for the artwork, you can use automated terrain and urban generation tools (which exist for most VR development platforms) to assist you with the process.
- VR software development process:
  - Custom VR software can be created using existing middleware platforms for game development such as Unity or Unreal. These platforms are typically available as free downloads for the development and testing of personal projects and allow for the adaptation of sample VR projects for your own VR experiences.

- Consider the use of preexisting VR platforms, such as OVAL (based on Unity), that can be repurposed for your own VR experiences. This approach can lower the technical barriers to creating custom VR experiences.
- Review the model/scene in VR and test on all headsets. Don't forget to make sure that all driver software is up-to-date before the event.

Program Instructions

Participants Day: This program can take the form of a field trip if held during normal school hours.

- Museum visit: First hour:
  - Students and teachers/adult supervisors will start at a museum. There, they will meet with one to two members of the museum's education/programming department and practice Close Looking—a method of observation and reflection that allows the students to use their imagination and use sketching and storytelling skills while looking at an object.

- Tech exploration at the library: Second hour:
  - This can involve moving to the tech area of your library, or, if you have mobile VR units, this could be brought to the museum.
  - During this part of the program, students are challenged to think about technology as a tool for understanding art.
  - Students receive a general overview of the VR and/or 3D scanning equipment they will be working with from one to two library personnel.
  - Students learn about and try to 3D scan an object (the Structure Sensor iPad scanner works well with people, and students often want to scan themselves).
  - Students will view/manipulate the artwork they spent the first hour studying in VR. If you have a larger group, consider having extra personnel nearby to help with any technical issues that may emerge.

- Lunch break

- Student creation project: Return to museum: Final portion (two to three hours):
  - Students will meet and work with the collaborator on a physical creation in the museum studio or classroom.
  - After seeing the artwork in physical and digital form, students will work together to realize their idea (one example would be building an environment for the ceramic pot they observed). Once our students complete the program, their creations are often put on display in either the library or museum.

RECOMMENDED NEXT PROJECTS

After your VR event is a success, it should be easy to use the experience you've gained to adapt the VR platform to incorporate different types of artwork. The materials needed and the workflow used can fit the subject matter that best fits your community's needs. Perhaps you have a popular science or natural history museum nearby you would prefer to use. Any "cost" incurred by the creation of the VR platform can thus be amortized over several VR events. Interested readers can also refer to other chapters in this book for useful information; e.g., chapter 21: "How to Create a VR Art Exhibition," chapter 4: "Leveraging VR Software to Create Virtual Art Exhibitions," and chapter 15: "Virtual Reality as a Medium for Community Art."

Keep It Clean
Essential Hygiene Practices for
Shared Head-Mounted Devices (HMDs)

BOBBY REED, Head of Emerging Technologies
University of Oklahoma Libraries

When worn, the average head-mounted device (HMD) comes in contact with ten square inches of the wearer's skin. The natural and violent human response to respiratory irritation means it is all too possible for a single sneeze or cough to contaminate the underside of the headset with "respiratory droplets"—a phrase that seemed unfamiliar to our cultural milieu until the outbreak of COVID. This new reality makes work dangerous for the library staff responsible for cleaning and for patrons who may come into contact with VR equipment in libraries. New practices must be enforced to move forward with emerging technologies, such as VR, while ensuring patron and staff safety.

Age Range	Type of Library Best Suited For	Cost Estimate
Kids (ages 3–7) Tweens (ages 8–12) Young adults (ages 13–18) Adults	Public libraries School libraries Academic libraries	Approximately $50 per month, plus a one-time cost of about $100 for a UVC cleaning light and safety goggles.

COST CONSIDERATIONS

If you are following any of the guides in this book, hygiene is not a consideration you can afford to miss. HMDs were hotbeds of unsanitary growth and bastions of bacteria before the global pandemic brought on by COVID. They are no different now, but the stakes are much higher for library staff and their patrons. The risks involved with not following proper cleaning protocols are unacceptable. With that in mind, if hygiene is not affordable, neither are HMDs.

OVERVIEW

In this new world, where viral infections can seem to suddenly creep up around the corner, we must ask ourselves: What methods can be utilized to keep HMDs clean and safe for shared use? By separating HMDs by use, using disposable headset covers, and cleaning and quarantining between uses with traditional cleaning and ultraviolet germicidal irradiation (UVGI) cleaning methods, libraries of all types can resume VR services and still provide a safe library experience.

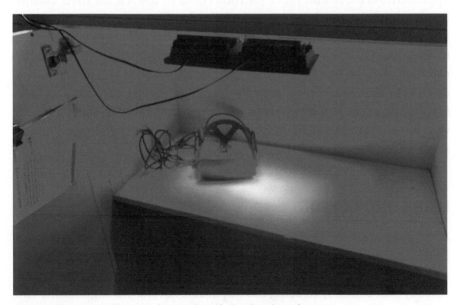

FIGURE 26.1 UVGI Cleaning of an Oculus Rift CV-1 headset after use

NECESSARY EQUIPMENT AND MATERIALS

- Disposable/washable covers
- UV-C Light 405nm (long exposure) or UV-C Light 254nm (short exposure but hazardous to humans)

STEP-BY-STEP INSTRUCTIONS

To kick this off, let's talk about the sweaty elephant in the room: Beat Saber. It is a neat and fun experience that inspires many folks to get up and move. In a country where heart disease remains high on the list of top killers, the use of this program is a clear positive. The smell that comes off our HMDs after Beat Saber has been played, however, is far from cool—which brings us to the first lesson: if possible, keep HMDs separated by use. This means the headset covered in sweat after a user finishes playing Robo Recall or The Climb stays sweaty and is the *only HMD* that can be used for heavily active games that result in a high risk of perspiration. If additional HMDs are simply not an option due to budget or space constraints, limiting usage time to prevent patrons from working up a sweat is an alternative approach. As more and more patrons come to use VR for their cardio, however, this approach increases in difficulty. That being said, librarians are the stewards of communal resources. If the use of one such resource is totally acceptable in a vacuum yet destroys the ability of others to have the same experience, that use is unacceptable. This is what we see in the case of VR apps that help you get your steps in or get your heart pumping. This is a great resource for one person. However, the reality is, sharing sweat with strangers is gross and unhygienic and something that library patrons should be protected against.

USING HMD COVERS

HMD covers come in disposable and washable offerings and can be purchased from major online retailers such as Amazon. Though washable covers typically fit HMDs better, patrons of OU Libraries' VR services prefer the mental security that comes with using the disposable covers. Throughout the two years we've spent regularly purchasing these at our institution, we've seen many manufacturers of these covers have come and gone. For this reason, the better practice is to check user reviews rather than specify a preferred vendor. Reading recent reviews on Amazon or Reddit will point you toward the companies that produce decent products at a decent price when you need to purchase them.

QUARANTINING

Recent advice published in the *Journal of Infectious Diseases* suggests that even in complete darkness, the SARS-CoV-2 virus suspended in saliva will lose viability after 125 minutes.[1] This is very promising news for the librarians around the globe trying to figure out how to keep patrons safe while still providing access to these technologies. According to the thinking in the article, quarantining HMDs after they are completely dry for at least 125 minutes is sufficient to prevent transmission of SARS-CoV-2. The dry portion here is incredibly important. To ensure that this quarantine method is effective, the HMD must be completely dry before the 125-minute clock starts.

CLEANLINESS COMMUNICATED

Regardless of your cleaning approach, always be informed and honest about the state of your gear. Headsets get gross (see the Beat Saber discussion above). If thirty-two undergraduate students or a class of middle schoolers have recently been in an HMD, let your patrons know. A librarian's duty isn't to make decisions for patrons but to provide access to the information and resources they need to make them the best decision-makers possible under the circumstances. This includes choosing whether to engage in risky, informed behavior. If a librarian cleans the headset with Lysol but didn't really saturate the foam, tell your patron that. The ethical duty to protect our patrons is nearly impossible to fulfill in our new, post-pandemic society. A library may still cease to function or a librarian fail to protect as best as they reasonably can and inform their patrons, allowing mitigation of their own risk. The end of the pandemic is not certain or in sight as of the time of this writing. This is in no way arguing that an effort shouldn't be made to clean HMDs between uses to make them as safe as possible. Rather, this is meant to point out that perfection in this health landscape is unreachable due to the constantly evolving information on the SARS-CoV-2 illness. By altering library practices to be safer, the world can slowly and cautiously resume the wonderful work it left behind in March 2020.

RECOMMENDED NEXT PROJECTS

Chapter 25: "ArtEdge: A Multidisciplinary Art and Tech VR Experience for School Children," put together by Kristi Wyatt, details an excellent first-development project that a librarian can replicate with the right organizational partners.

NOTE

1. Michael Schuit et al., "Airborne SARS-CoV-2 Is Rapidly Inactivated by Simulated Sunlight," *The Journal of Infectious Diseases* 222, no. 4 (August 2020): 564–71, https://doi.org/10.1093/infdis/jiaa334.

VR Orientation on a Light Budget
Library Orientation for New University Students Using Inexpensive Virtual Reality Technology

SANDRA VALENTI, Assistant Professor

TING WANG, PhD student and Research Assistant

BRADY LUND, PhD student and Research Assistant

Emporia State University, Kansas

The purpose of this project is to develop an engaging alternative to the traditional library orientation offered to first-time library users through the use of virtual reality technology. While in-person library orientation may still be the first choice of many library employees and users, events such as the 2020 COVID-19 pandemic demonstrate that this is not always a practical possibility. In the fall 2020 semester, many students entered the university without the opportunity to participate in any library orientation due to social distancing policies that restricted gathering in groups. This VR alternative, in addition to offering an exciting new way to engage students wherever they are, simulates a tour through the library environment as closely as possible when a physical orientation is not feasible.

This VR orientation can include many elements one would expect from a traditional library orientation/tour: an introduction to the facilities and employees, a discussion of the various services the library offers . . . even a little information literacy instruction. The only major difference is that the physical world is eschewed in favor of the virtual!

Age Range	Type of Library Best Suited For	Cost Estimate
Young adults (ages 13–18) Adults	Public libraries School libraries Academic libraries	0–$1,000

COST CONSIDERATIONS

The cost for this project includes the purchase of a VR camera (the Samsung Gear 360, which sells for about $300, was used in the case study that inspired this chapter) and Google cardboard viewers (at about $3 per viewer). If your library is part of a university, school, or large library system, one of the other departments may have a VR camera available that you could borrow. Additionally, you might ask students to purchase their own viewer (however, it would then be difficult to ensure all students will receive the same opportunity to participate in the experience if they are all required to bring their own equipment). All other necessary materials (video editors, VR development software, etc.) can be found for free online.

OVERVIEW

With this project, libraries can design, develop, and distribute a VR experience that orients users to the library environment and services. Initially, the development will be quite similar to any library orientation: The developer of the VR experience will identify key information about the library, its services, and its people that should be communicated to new library users. However, when this information has been collected, it is not just stored until such time that a group of new users visit the library. Instead, it is incorporated into an

FIGURE 27.1
Virtual orientation to library

interactive VR experience that, similar to directing a movie, requires additional forethought and a little bit of talent behind a camera. There is a bit of a learning curve in developing this type of VR experience, but the difficulty lies more in learning how to operate behind (and around) a camera than in dealing with any technological hassles. When this project is complete, you should have an artifact that can be shared on websites (such as with Google Maps) and through mobile VR (headsets) and be a truly distinguishing element of your library's service.

NECESSARY EQUIPMENT AND MATERIALS

- Video camera—a phone camera will be sufficient; quality may vary.
- VR camera and any software or apps required to operate it—the packaging of the camera will specify what is needed.
- Google Cardboard or a similar VR headset
- VeeR VR (veer.tv) platform (free VR software) or a similar VR platform

Recommended but Optional Materials

- Tripod (inexpensive and very helpful)
- Video (not VR) editor

STEP-BY-STEP INSTRUCTIONS

Preparation

- Develop a plan that includes all the information you would like to include in your VR experience as well as the locations within the library you would like to incorporate as part of the VR experience. Examples include a tour of the facility, LibGuides and databases, staff introductions, and meeting and computing spaces.
- Ensure the VR camera you are using is charged and set up according to the manufacturer's directions.
- Take the VR camera to the areas you want to include in the VR experience and experiment with the technology and the appearance of the space/images. If you do not want to be in the picture, make sure you are out of range of the camera (most VR cameras are operated using a smartphone

app for this purpose). You may want to hide behind a tree if you are out-doors or go to another room if you are indoors.

- If there are web-based sources you would like to include in the experience, such as a tutorial on how to use the library's database, a screen capture tool can be used to record video.
- For any people you want to include in the experience (e.g., interviews with subject librarians, reference services personnel, library adminis-tration), use a regular camera; VR does not work well for this purpose if you expect users to focus their attention on the speaker.
- When all the images/video have been recorded, follow the directions with the VR camera to upload the content to a computer.
- Upload the pictures to VeeR VR or a similar VR editing platform and drag-and-drop interactive elements, including text boxes, videos, audios, and transitions to connect all the pictures.
- VeeR VR (and several similar platforms) offers the capacity to make your VR experience available as a desktop application (such as Google Maps) and mobile application (compatible with both phones and tablets). However, the mobile application is not available in an app store; rather, the users will need to visit the web address for the VR experience in their browser of choice and then select an option that enables a mobile experience. It is a good idea to have all employees who interact with the public experiment with this technology so that they can assist patrons who may have questions.
- Make an instruction booklet on how to find and use the VR experience (you may also add this information on the library's website).

Engage

- If funding offers the opportunity to distribute a headset to all incoming students, this would be an ideal way to reach the intended audience. If not, then promotion through university communication avenues may help the experience reach students who can either use a headset they already own or purchase one at their expense.
- It is important to educate users about potential health and safety risks with VR technology (e.g., warn patrons regarding the possibility of motion sickness, ensure the space is clear of obstacles so users can enjoy the expe-rience in a space without tripping over or running into anything, etc.).

Explore

- Help participants navigate their VR experience through e-mail, video conference, or chat, if necessary.
- Prepare to adjust the VR experience, if necessary, based on users' feedback. It is useful to "beta test" the VR experience by sending it to a small group of students and then soliciting feedback to refine the experience.

Empower

- This preliminary experience with VR in the semi-structured environment of library orientation serves also as an orientation to VR technology. Users may gain some competency in the use of VR and decide to explore other VR opportunities offered by the library or other organizations.
- Allow feedback from the VR experience to guide the development of future VR projects.

LEARNING OUTCOMES

Participants will:

- Develop an understanding of the physical layout of the library environment and the programs and services the library offers
- Experience increased clarity and reduced anxiety about what the library is, who works there, and who can/does use it
- Acquire knowledge and experience with VR technology, which may translate to other VR opportunities that the library offers

RECOMMENDED NEXT PROJECTS

- In academic libraries: For special collections/exhibitions, consider using a VR experience that will capture the authentic feel of the exhibits; this can be helpful for researchers and students around the world who are interested in your collections.
- In school libraries: Download educational VR mobile apps on other topics; for instance, introduction to the solar system and to body structure to help students increase their learning motivation.

- In public libraries: Build a VR experience that familiarizes patrons to your institution's physical structure and that introduces all your librarians, which will serve to reduce patron library-related anxiety and increase their willingness to visit the library to seek the information they need.

Using VR In Youth Programming

HOLLY EBERLE, Youth Technology Librarian

Algonquin Area Public Library District, Illinois

Using virtual reality in your youth programming can allow kids to see countries all over the globe, learn about different careers, visit a college campus, or explore a brand new topic in an immersive way. Library workers can use VR technology as the focal point of a program or to enhance one. This is also an easy technology to take outside of the library for outreach services within the community.

Another fun way to use VR is with pop-up programming. You never know who is at your library! For example, one day, during winter break, I did a pop-up Staycation VR program using the Google Expeditions for Argentina. Some boys came up to try the VR, then exclaimed to me that their au-pair was from Argentina. They dragged her over; she was very excited, almost tearful, to see the VR version of Buenos Aires. It was a great library moment made possible with VR technology.

The possibilities for library programming with this technology are nearly limitless. Library workers may use them in STEM programs, literacy programs, geography programs, or just for fun, nonacademic programs. VR Technology is also great for intergenerational programming. It is not just for kids, and oftentimes parents and grandparents are extremely interested in trying it out with their children.

Age Range	Type of Library Best Suited For	Cost Estimate
Tweens (ages 8–12) Young Adults (ages 13-18)	Public libraries School libraries	$4,000

COST CONSIDERATIONS

There is a high upfront cost for the 10-Pack Google Expeditions Student VR Kit, which our library purchased from Best Buy. Once you make this investment, the kit may be used for many different purposes. Never doubt your ability to secure a grant either!

OVERVIEW

What makes the Google Expeditions Student VR Kit so great is its versatility. Library workers can plan for the VR viewers to be the main focus of a program, or they may choose to enhance a non-technology program using VR viewers.

If the plan is to focus on the VR viewers alone, I would recommend a thirty- to forty-five-minute program. If the plan is to enhance another program, I would plan for at least fifteen minutes for use of the VR viewers. This type of program does not need many staff members; I would say no more than one or two people is sufficient. Depending on the size of your program, you may need more staff members to monitor attendees, but the technology is easy enough for one person to handle.

The size of your groups will be limited to how many VR viewers your library owns. I only have ten, but you can explore options to purchase sets of fifteen or thirty viewers. I have found that drop-in or pop-up VR programming is a wonderful way for library users to get a taste of the technology. In such programs, you can maximize your program numbers since people will be sharing the viewers and then moving along afterward.

VR is fun for the whole family, though I would not recommend a VR program for children below the second grade without an accompanying adult present. I have done a kindergarten-through-second-grade VR program before, but it was a bit of an uncontrollable disaster. You may also need to gently remind children that they are still on planet Earth and can run into real-life things such as bookshelves, walls, or other kids. VR is really cool, but it is easy to get caught up in!

Some people have reported vertigo or nauseousness after looking into the viewers. I noticed a little bit of this myself, but it was something I was able to get used to and no longer experience. If a child is experiencing this, let them know that it is totally normal and that the feeling should pass if they take a break from the viewer. However, I have noticed this complaint more from adults than children.

NECESSARY EQUIPMENT AND MATERIALS

- 10-Pack Google Expeditions Student VR Kit (which accommodates ten students)
- Microfiber cloth
- Alcohol-based cleaner for VR viewers

STEP-BY-STEP INSTRUCTIONS

Preparation

- Make sure that all Android phones and the teacher tablet are charged. Chargers are included in the kit.
- Turn on the kit's teacher tablet, connect to your local Wi-Fi, create a Google account, and download the Google Expeditions app. Ensure you are recognized by the software as the teacher guide by selecting the *Lead* button. Download the Expeditions you would like onto your tablet. Google has compiled a spreadsheet detailing their available Expeditions. The title of this spreadsheet is "Expeditions - List of Available Expeditions." A simple Google search for "Google Expeditions list" will retrieve this.
- Plug in the kit's router and turn it on.
- Make sure the teacher tablet is connected to the kit's wireless network.
- Turn on the VR viewer phones and open the Expeditions app. The student devices will see the viewer screen by default. Make sure that each student's device is placed inside their VR viewer headset.

- If you have used the VR viewers previously, clean the eye area out with an alcohol-based solution to avoid germs or infections such as pinkeye.

Program Instructions

- Place your VR viewers out for use. Press *Play* on the teacher tablet when you are ready to begin playing your first Expedition. To change slides for the students, swipe to the right and press *Play* on the following slide.
- The Expeditions app gives you some fun facts about the places or things your students are looking at. You can point them in the direction of something you want them all to focus on as well.

RECOMMENDED NEXT PROJECTS

Google Cardboard is an easy next step after you have used your first VR app. While Expeditions offers a good introduction to VR technology, Cardboard allows for more interactive and immersive VR experiences. Cardboard is a separate app and not affiliated with the Expeditions app.

Another cool next step would be to have the students create their own VR tours using Google's Tour Creator tool. Finally, in addition to offering a VR experience, Expeditions has an augmented reality (AR) component as well. Google has compiled a list of available AR Expeditions in the same spreadsheet as the VR Expeditions; the AR options are just located in a different tab.

Adapting to COVID-19
Transitioning a Library Orientation Game Night to an Enhanced Virtual Tour

MEGAN WILSON, Research and Instruction Librarian/Assistant Professor

JEFF HENRY, Research and Instruction Librarian/Associate Professor

Murray State University, Kentucky

n today's environment, it can be difficult to host some traditional in-person library activities. Library game nights or tours can be challenging to facilitate while adhering to social distancing protocols and possible library capacity issues. One way of overcoming these obstacles is by developing a virtual tour enhanced by embedded games and activities. Participants can explore and familiarize themselves with the physical spaces of your library as they learn about important policies, people, and resources associated with select locations within your library, all while enjoying some embedded games and activities to make it fun and educational! The program is an entertaining and innovative way to adapt the traditional in-person library tour to a fun, virtual experience. The limits of this program are set only by your imagination.

Age Range	Type of Library Best Suited For	Cost Estimate
Tweens (ages 8–12) Young adults (ages 13–18) Adults	Public libraries School libraries Academic libraries	$200–$800

COST CONSIDERATIONS

Cost is dependent on the equipment used. A 360 camera is highly recommended but not required. These tour programs vary in price, with free and freemium versions available along with more expensive options. Cost may also be dependent on the number of panoramas included and the software used.

OVERVIEW

In this project, participants will be able to explore library spaces through a virtual 360 tour. The tour is enhanced by adding a variety of hotspots that can include information, photos, and videos about collections, policies, locations, and people as well as a selection of games and activities. You may be familiar with your library, but as you know, many patrons are not. Your tour can integrate all the information you feel your participants should know about your library, or at the very least, answer some of your patrons' most frequently asked questions. Your tour can be as robust and informative as you feel is necessary for your library's needs. Likewise, the embedded games within your tour can be custom-selected to fit your audience and requirements. For instance, if cost and privacy are priorities for your library, you could choose to utilize only free online games that do not require participants to register or download anything.

FIGURE 29.1
Virtual tour of
library

Staffing needs for your project will depend on how expansive your tour will be and other job obligations that those assisting in its creation might have. At the least, you should have one person devoted to the project so that they can dedicate themselves to learning how to operate the camera and the software and an additional person devoted to the embedded content within the tour. Once the project is completed, no staffing should be required unless updates or modifications are required or wanted. Additionally, the online asynchronous nature of the program does not require limiting the number of users who can participate at any given time.

NECESSARY EQUIPMENT AND MATERIALS

- Camera and picture editing software
- Computer
- Tour creation software

Recommended but Optional Materials

- 360 camera

STEP-BY-STEP INSTRUCTIONS

Preparation

- Decide how you want to create your tour; panoramas can be taken with phone apps or stitched together with traditional photos, but a 360 camera is highly recommended due to its ease of use.
- Research and familiarize yourself with the tour software that you choose for your project. The choice of software will likely depend on such factors as cost, resources, and degree of functionality. Free programs such as Google's Tour Creator are more limited in scope, and some creators, such as Marzipano, require the user to have a server on which to host the tour. Other considerations may include the ease of editing after the fact.
- Predetermine areas to use as hotspots within the tour to ensure they are visible in the images for the tour, keeping in mind that objects will seem further away in the photos than they are in reality from the same location.

Program Instructions

- Design the tour by first choosing major points of interest; this may include areas such as the circulation desk, printers, or student services. You may also wish to highlight certain collections such as games or popular reading.
- Select your locations to photograph; test shots are highly recommended to make sure that all the selected reference points are clearly visible.
- Take your photographs; use of the HDR camera setting is highly recommended to get the best light exposure.
    - If you are using a traditional camera, you will need to stitch together a panorama using postediting software.
    - Taking extra images at various viewpoints is highly recommended to avoid any reshoots later.
- Upload the panoramas to the tour software of your choice.
- Use the tour software to link the panoramas and introduce hotspots. The methodology for this will vary based on the software used but is typically done through a drag-and-drop system.
    - Note that some programs, such as Theasys and Pannek, allow the use of different icons for additional customization; others, such as Google's Tour creator, are more limited.
- Select the games and activities to be embedded.
    - The games that you select for your tour can be anything available online; however, you may want to consider cost, privacy, and limitations of access when selecting the games to include. You may also want the games to correlate with the locations of the hotspots within your tour; for example, you could embed a geography game near a map collection. The most important thing is for the games to be fun and engaging.
- Select information to be embedded at the major physical points of interest.
    - Suggested content may include information that exists on your website's "about us" page. You can also include contact information as well as tutorials on using certain resources and technology.
    - Note that depending on the program used, photographs, videos, and hyperlinks may also be embedded for additional interaction.

- Set up hotspots for games and the points of interest within the tour and embed the content.
  - Informational content should be embedded in clear proximity to the location that the information pertains to. Links to games and activities may be placed anywhere in the tour; however, spacing them out between panoramas may encourage participants to explore them in-depth.
- Publish the tour to make it live. Options for embedment may vary depending on the program used and whether the tour is hosted online or locally.
- Market the tour to your patrons.
  - Consider including the tour with other promotional or orientation programming offered to new patrons. The tour can also be a useful tool for introducing new renovations and/or additions to your library.
- Measure the impact of your program using web analytics and other metrics.

RECOMMENDED NEXT PROJECTS

If your project has experienced success, you can enhance it further by embedding in-house created games to make the experience more customized. Consider creating a virtual escape room that incorporates resources and information about your library or a scavenger hunt utilizing the virtual tour and requiring the use of your library's resources. Another option would be to embed links to live events during scheduled times to add a synchronous element and/or promote community engagement.

Create an AR Game Based on Your Library's Catalog System

JULIA UHR, PhD student at the ATLAS Institute

University of Colorado Boulder

n this chapter, you'll learn how to make an augmented reality (AR) game that will help players navigate your library's catalog system. This AR program takes the form of a scavenger hunt game that gives players a series of call numbers where they can find different AR markers. When viewed through a phone camera, 3D objects appear on top of the markers. Players can collect an object by clicking on it, after which the game immediately gives them a new call number. They win by collecting all the objects. This project involves some coding, but no prior coding experience is necessary to complete the game.

Age Range	Type of Library Best Suited For	Cost Estimate
Kids (ages 3–7) Tweens (ages 8–12) Young adults (ages 13–18) Adults	Public libraries Academic libraries	$0–$50

OVERVIEW

The following sections will walk you through the process of setting up a website for the game, adding template code to the site, customizing the

FIGURE 30.1 Marker 2 viewed through a smartphone

Collected 0/3
First stop: JK 1976.S43 2001

code, setting up the AR markers, and playing the game. It will initially take about two hours to set up the website and place the markers. After the website is working, players will be able to access the game on their own devices and play independently. The code and markers required for this project can be found in the associated GitHub repository at https://github.com/juliauhr/Library-AR-Game.

NECESSARY EQUIPMENT AND MATERIALS

- Printed paper markers
- Wireless internet access
- Phones, tablets, or laptops (players will need to bring in their own)

STEP-BY-STEP INSTRUCTIONS

Make the Game Website

The web page for your game can be a page on your library's website or hosted on a platform, such as GitHub Pages or Glitch, as long as it uses HTTPS. The following instructions are for Glitch because it's easy to use and will work for anyone.

- First, start a new Glitch project.
  - Go to https://glitch.com. Glitch is a free tool that makes it easy to build and host websites.
  - Click *new project*, then *hello webpage*, which will create a new website with default content.

- Change the URL of your site. In the upper-left corner will be some random words, such as "cottony-fluff-increase," which is the current name of your project. Click on the name to change it. This will also change the URL of your site.
- Delete all the files except the one labeled *index.html*. On the left side, there is a list of files. Click on the three dots next to the file name to delete it. You should be left with the files: *index.html* and *assets*.
- Open *index.html* by clicking on it.
- Delete everything in the *index.html* file.
- Next, add the template code to your *index.html* file. This can be found in the GitHub repository at https://github.com/juliauhr/Library-AR-Game/blob/master/index.html. Next, copy and paste the template code into your *index.html* file.

Print the Markers

- Find the sheet with the barcode markers numbered 0, 1, 2, 3, and 4 at https://github.com/juliauhr/Library-AR-Game/blob/master/markers.pdf.
- Print the sheet.
- Cut the sheet into pieces with one marker on each piece. For now, you will only need markers 0, 1, 2.

Test Your Game

- Test your website on a computer or device with a camera.
    - If you are working on a computer with a camera, you can view your website by clicking on *show* and *in a new window*.
    - If your computer does not have a camera, use a phone or other device with a camera and view your website by going to https://[your site's name].glitch.me.
- When prompted, give the site access to your camera.
- You should see the image from your camera and text at the bottom that says, *Collected 0/3*, *First stop*, and a call number.
- Hold one of the markers up to the camera. You should see a rotating sphere over the marker.
- Click on the sphere. It should shrink. The "collected" total should change to 1/3, and the call number should change.

- Hold the other two markers up to the camera. They should each show a differently colored sphere. When you've clicked on all three spheres, the text should tell you that you found them all.

Customize the Code

- Decide how many items you want to include in your scavenger hunt (in the code, these are called "collectibles") and which call numbers you want to place them at.
- Add all your collectibles to the code.
  - Toward the middle of the code in *index.html*, find the three code blocks starting with *collectibles.push*. These are the three default shapes. You can add more shapes by copying one of these blocks.
  - To change a collectible's call number, change its *callNumber* attribute.
  - To change the shape of a collectible, change the *shape* attribute from *a-sphere* to *a-box*, *a-cone*, *a-torus*, or some other shape.
  - To change a collectible's material (the image displayed on the shape):
    » First, go to the *assets* folder for your Glitch project and upload the image you want to use.
    » Second, copy the URL of the uploaded image and paste it into the collectible's *material* attribute.
- There are many other attributes you can change, including scale, position, rotation, and animation. You can also combine multiple shapes for a single marker. To learn more, go to https://aframe.io.

Print and Place the Markers

- Print a marker for each of your collectibles. Each marker must be unique. If you need more markers than provided on the marker sheet on GitHub, you can make more using a marker-generator such as the one at https://au.gmented.com/app/marker/marker.php.
- Cut out the markers and place them in the location in your library's book stacks defined by the collectible's call number. Make sure the order of the markers matches the order of the collectibles; so, in our example, Marker 0 is at the call number location of the first collectible, Marker 1 is at the location of the second collectible, and so on.

Play the Game

- Once everything is set up, play through the whole game to make sure it works.
- Encourage visitors to your library to play the game by posting links on your website, posting fliers with QR codes, or organizing groups of kids to play together.

Troubleshooting

- Make sure players are accessing your game using an address starting with "https://." The game won't work using HTTP.
- For the game to work on a specific device, the web browser must have access to the device's camera; so, players may need to change their app settings to give their browser app permission to use the camera.
- A-Frame and AR.js are updated regularly, so your code may wind up being out-of-date at some point. You can find up-to-date code at https://github.com/juliauhr/Library-AR-Game.

RECOMMENDED NEXT PROJECTS

You can find other programs you might try at your library in the following chapters in this book:

- Chapter 8: "How to Create Augmented Reality Culture Expedition Experiences"
- Chapter 16: "Augmented Reality Introduction for Libraries: Metaverse and Library Services"
- Chapter 18: "Amazin' Creations: Augmented Reality Critter Creation Tutorial"

Keepin' It Real
Piloting AR, VR, and MR in the Library

JOLANDA-PIETA VAN ARNHEM, Scholars Studio Librarian
ELENA RODRIGUEZ, Instruction Coordinator
College of Charleston, South Carolina

T he VR Classroom Instruction Lending Program provides college students the opportunity to experience virtual reality in their regularly scheduled courses. With the help of librarian and faculty collaboration, standard lessons can be transformed into meaningful and exciting experiences that allow students to ask big questions and discuss big answers. It also gives students the chance to play with types of technology they may not normally have access to. Even though the fields of VR and augmented reality (AR) are rapidly evolving, programs such as this can be adapted to fit a variety of budgets and audiences to provide exciting spaces for engagement in learning.

The Library Freshman Seminar AR U Experienced: An Introduction to Augmented and Virtual Reality provides college students with the opportunity to experience a credit-bearing, research-focused library course as part of the First Year Experience (FYE) program. In this course, students examine the technologies behind AR and VR and explore their history and societal effects. These experiences provide students with a unique opportunity to experience VR on a weekly basis and use those experiences to evaluate the relevance, quality, and appropriateness of different sources of information. This semester-long instruction exposes students to a variety of forms of information/visual literacy. The course is designed to teach and demonstrate some of the basic tools of analysis and critical thinking with which to approach contemporary texts presented through the lens of augmented and virtual realities.

Age Range	Type of Library Best Suited For	Cost Estimate
Young adults (ages 13–18) Adults	Academic libraries	$300–$13,000-plus (based on twenty seats)

COST CONSIDERATIONS

- Google Cardboard using personal devices and headphones/earbuds: $300
- Merge Headset using personal devices and headphones/earbuds: $1,000
- Google Expeditions VR Classroom Kit 20-Student Pack and headphones (headset/device/router; rolling cart not included): $6,000
- Mid-range wireless headset with charging/storage cart and headphones: $13,000

OVERVIEW

The VR Classroom Instruction Lending Program is designed for librarians and faculty to collaborate to provide an immersive learning experience for students and to champion inclusion and accessibility to emerging technologies. VR, AR, and 360 videos are making the transition from gaming at home to in the classroom. The 2019 Horizon Report for Higher Education

FIGURE 31.1   AR, VR, and MR at Addlestone Library

reports that the increased use of AR, VR, and mixed reality (MR) has enabled mobile learning to become more active and collaborative, providing unique opportunities to enhance established learning models.

The program is offered in the fall and spring semesters, though to limit burnout, capping the number of sessions or faculty members you work with is advisable, particularly in the piloting phase. The number of VR sessions you set up with a faculty member should be negotiated based on librarian and headset availability. While the group size will vary depending on the amount of equipment you have available, groups of twenty or less are easier to manage and assist. To help with troubleshooting and classroom questions, you should have at least one other person to assist in the classroom.

The Library Freshman Seminar builds on the goals of the VR Classroom Instruction Lending Program and provides additional opportunities for students to engage in an interactive learning environment focused on library research as part of the First Year Experience (FYE) program. The semester-long instruction is offered in the fall and spring semesters. Student participation is capped at twenty students, which is consistent with the FYE program guidelines. To work in tandem with the VR Classroom Instruction Lending Program, class times during which the VR headsets can be used are scheduled in blocks, and all VR instruction sessions are delivered in the same room. This room has been configured to display the headsets through a projection screen using Google Chrome.

Classroom management for the Library Freshman Seminar students is essential. Students are provided an overview on how to use and navigate the headsets on the first day of class. Each activity is demonstrated using the class projection system. Student volunteers assist each other during activities to troubleshoot and ask questions. Activities often involve working in groups or teams. Each student is assigned their own unique headset, controller, and headphones for the duration of the semester and is responsible for picking up their headsets at the beginning of class. At the end of class, each student is required to sanitize and return their headset to the charging cart located in the classroom. It is advisable to double-check all the headsets at the end of each class to ensure that they are all put in the correct numbered slots and are connected to the charging station.

Learning Outcomes

- As instructional content may vary, course-specific learning outcomes will also need to be considered. In the context of using VR headsets, however, participants will:
- Analyze ideas and ways VR supports their learning
- Demonstrate the ability to navigate emerging technologies related to VR, AR, and MR
- Evaluate the relevance, quality, and appropriateness of different sources of information
- Use appropriate critical-thinking skills and problem-solving techniques in appropriate disciplinary contexts to make connections across disciplines and/or relevant experiences

NECESSARY EQUIPMENT AND MATERIALS

- VR headsets of your choice
- A room or dedicated space, along with tables and chairs, with access to the internet and a projector
- Headphones
- Google Chromecast
- Sanitizing wipes
- Disposable facemasks

STEP-BY-STEP INSTRUCTIONS
Preparation

- Investigate faculty and academic program interest on your campus, both formally and informally.
- Research the current technology available based on your program's budget and purchase the necessary associated equipment.
- Clearly number and identify all headsets and equipment, including chargers, headphones, controllers, etc.
- If using a stand-alone headset, configure a shared account to link to the headsets.
- If using a smartphone VR headset, ensure the headset is adjustable to fit a wide variety of phones.

- You may also need to consider providing students with mobile devices.
- Decide if your program will be mobile or if you will have a designated classroom space.
  - A designated classroom space allows for easier troubleshooting regarding connectivity and other known variables, though a mobile approach may allow for more flexible instruction.
- Generate a Use Proposal Form for faculty and/or your academic programs and provide any other necessary information.
  - Be sure to clarify the guidelines for the program on the form; you may also want to consider creating a LibGuide.
  - Be sure to research the necessary steps for creating and delivering a for-credit course at your institution.
  - You may want to start with a VR Classroom Instruction Lending Program and then expand your efforts to include a Library Freshman Seminar/credit-bearing library course.
- Decide who will be on the proposal review panel.
  - We recommend you select one or two instruction librarians and, if available, a library system support manager or comparable staff member.
  - If you are creating a Library Freshman Seminar/credit-bearing library course, you may want to include members of your library administration. You will need their approval on the course proposal and for the curriculum submission process.

Program Instructions

VR Classroom Instruction Lending Program

Faculty Collaboration

- Circulate the proposal form to faculty.
  - In the pilot stage, send the form to faculty in a phased approach, especially if you are limiting the number of sessions you are offering in the program.
- Proposal submissions will be evaluated and approved by the VR Library Instruction proposal review panel to ensure the request can be handled.
- Share the proposal with the appropriate liaison librarian invited to lead the session.

- Whoever is set to lead the instruction session should contact faculty to confirm dates and then invite them to meet to discuss the plans for the session.
- Enlist one other person for the program to assist the day of the session.

Day of Session

- Set up the room twenty minutes prior to the session's start to account for any technical difficulties.
  - This includes but is not limited to setting up the Google Chromecast display, laying out headsets for students, powering headsets on, and making sure all remotes are properly synched.
- Once students and faculty have arrived, gauge their familiarity using VR headsets before describing the headsets to be used in the session.
- Provide some disclaimers and rules. We suggest the following, but you should consider the guidelines in place with your program and recommended by your department:
  - No photos while the headsets are on unless you have the user's expressed permission
  - If at any time a student feels ill, please remove the headset.
  - If anyone has any questions, please raise a hand; touch them on the shoulder when you are next to them to let them know you are there to assist.
  - Ask for their consideration when you request they remove their headsets to rejoin the class.
- Lead the students through an introductory demo to get them acquainted with their headsets before the actual lesson plan. Five to ten minutes on this portion of the program is recommended.
  - If your headset is capable, connecting to Chromecast is a valuable way to show students what to expect and how to navigate the software.
  - Ask students to take off their headsets once they have completed the introduction.
- After the demo, conduct your lesson plan as designed with the faculty member.
- At the end of your session, hand students sanitizing wipes to clean off their headsets before returning them to your storage cart (or other storage solution).

- Ensure all equipment is properly stored, charging, and/or secured for your next VR session!

Library Freshman Seminar

Faculty Collaboration

- Investigate academic program interest on your campus; include discussions with faculty administration. You will need their approval for designing the course, submitting the course proposal, and for the curriculum submission process.
- Identify a lead course instructor or instruction team and technology assistant.
- Review guidelines for creating a new course proposal. Establish time lines and responsibilities. Draft a course proposal for review by the VR Library Instruction proposal review panel to ensure that the request can be handled and that the course learning outcomes are in line with the department/program. Revise the proposal based on feedback.
- Share/submit the proposal using the appropriate institutional processes. If approved, work with the appropriate departments/programs to schedule/deliver your courses.

Semester Sessions

- Prior to class, load any necessary apps or create class playlists.
- Set up the laptop cart (or another program option you selected) in the room twenty minutes prior to the session's start to account for any technical difficulties.
  - This includes but is not limited to setting up the Google Chromecast display and checking for uncharged headsets, missing headsets, or remotes.
- During the first week of class, assign headsets and provide students with an overview on how to use them. This includes how to download apps, general setup guidelines, and common troubleshooting tips that are demonstrated using the class projection system.
- Provide the same disclaimers and rules that are used for the VR Classroom Instruction Lending Program sessions (see above).

- Request that student volunteers assist each other during activities to troubleshoot and answer questions.
- Review the format for instruction and during class activities. Provide instructions and responsibilities for picking up headsets at the beginning of class. Demonstrate how each student is required to sanitize and return their headset to the charging cart located in the classroom at the end of class.
- Conduct your lesson plan.
- At the end of your session, hand students sanitizing wipes to clean off their headsets before returning them to your storage cart (or other storage solution).
- Ensure all equipment is properly stored, charging, and/or secured for your next VR session!

RECOMMENDED NEXT PROJECTS

You can find a lot of new ideas on how to create fun and interesting AR/VR lesson plans and make them meaningful and exciting experiences in your VR Classroom Instruction Lending Program and/or Library Freshman Seminar. See the following chapters for inspiration:

- Chapter 2: "Creating Dynamic, Immersive Field Trips with ClassVR and ThingLink"
- Chapter 18: "Amazin' Creations: Augmented Reality Critter Creation Tutorial"
- Chapter 21: "How to Create a VR Art Exhibition"

Adventures in VR
Mobile Virtual Reality Events for the 50+ Community

ERIK ROCK, Library Technology and Innovation Lead
DANIELLE STEPHENS, Library Aide
Loveland Public Library, Colorado

A s an emerging technology, virtual reality provides fully immersive, lifelike adventures in a safe, controlled space with little to no risk involved. Participants can experience scenarios and environments they would not typically get the chance to explore. This is particularly true for the fifty-plus community, who may have impaired physical abilities or ability to travel. Not only is VR a fun leisure activity, but it also improves cognitive function, increases empathy, helps with memory retention and recall, and can help improve balance and equilibrium. Despite the benefits, engaging the fifty-plus community with VR can be a challenge due to sociocultural factors and overall hesitation toward technology. However, engaging the fifty-plus community with VR can be possible when you bring the VR opportunities to them! By making your VR station fully mobile, you can increase your technology outreach, easily change locations, and engage with patrons, such as those in the fifty-plus community, who otherwise would not come into a library building or a typical library technology event.

Age Range	Type of Library Best Suited For	Cost Estimate
Adults Seniors (50+)	Public libraries	$1,000–$4,500

COST CONSIDERATIONS

Cost is dependent on several factors, including the number of units your library wishes to have, whether you want all-in-one or PC-powered VR stations, your program's mobility, and so forth. All-in-One VR units, such as the Oculus Quest, range between $399 to $499 per unit but have resolution, speed, and range limitations. Full-resolution, high-quality PC-powered VR units, such as Oculus Rift S ($399), can be made mobile by installing a mid-range gaming PC (approximately $999 to $1,500) to a mobile, rolling laptop and TV cart (approximately $100 to $199). VR sensors and speakers can be mounted on the cart using selfie-sticks (approximately $10 to $25) or zip-ties ($5). Power via an uninterrupted battery power supply (approximately $130 to $200) can be similarly mounted to make the cart fully mobile. Though a significant investment, PC-powered VR programming offers better quality and higher resolution than less costly alternatives.

OVERVIEW

An off-site VR program with a PC-powered VR headset on a mobile cart can be transported and moved to multiple locations. Developing a successful VR event for the fifty-plus community using a mobile VR station involves taking

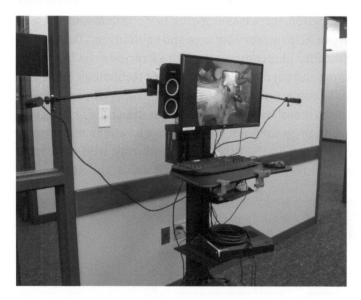

FIGURE 32.1
Oculus Rift headset, sensors, and gaming PC mounted to a mobile, rolling laptop cart.

the station off-site to a community location that specializes in outreach to the fifty-plus community or partnering with such an organization to bring outside participants into the library. While a VR program for the fifty-plus community can be hosted on-site at your library, taking the mobile cart offsite to community partners or organizations that specialize in outreach to this patron demographic will ensure engagement and act as a technology outreach solution. Offering a VR technology program specifically will help participants experience, learn, and have fun with the technology without as many of the hurdles that can occur when having events for all ages. Many cultural factors can cause hesitation or disinterest in adults fifty-plus regarding using emerging technology. Demonstrating to the older community that VR can be both valuable *and* fun is possible when you bring the VR to them at a location they are familiar with. Staff involvement will be somewhat high for participants completely new to VR; this level of involvement is necessary to allow them to gain expertise with the hardware/software and to ensure that participants in the program are comfortable enough to use it. A program of this nature should have a duration of sixty to 120 minutes to give each participant enough time to use the VR station.

NECESSARY EQUIPMENT AND MATERIALS

- Oculus Rift S headsets and controllers
- Accompanying Oculus and/or Steam account(s)
- A selection of installed VR games, videos, and simulations
- Mobile cart to transport the gaming PC, VR headset, and so forth
- Gaming PC
- Speakers

Recommended but Optional Materials

- Extra batteries (for controllers)
- Bottled water
- Chairs
- Snacks
- Projector
- HDMI cable(s)

- Fatigue mat
- Hand sanitizer for participants to use before touching the equipment
- Disinfectant wipes to clean the equipment between participants
- Baskets or mounts to hold the controllers, batteries, wipes, and so forth

STEP-BY-STEP INSTRUCTIONS

Preparation

- Assembly of the mobile Oculus VR carts will take about three to four hours per station; this time frame includes assembly of the mobile cart, configuring the PC and performing software updates, hooking up the headset components and organizing the wires, and installing the necessary apps such as Oculus and Steam VR.
- Ensure you have an Oculus and Steam account set up; an Oculus for Business account is preferred as it gives you warranty options and increased customer support.
- Download the games directly in the Oculus and Steam apps. Test them thoroughly.
- Consider the types of VR experiences that may be interesting for your community members but avoid making assumptions about "ability" levels based on age. Tours, video simulations, and observational games tend to go over better with beginners than games that require a lot of patron control over game functions/options.
- Ensure you have a variety of VR games, experiences, and tours to choose from, including selections at different levels (novice, beginner, intermediate, advanced). Consider experiences that can take place in both a seated and standing position as well as those with sound versus no sound.
- Staff must have the necessary expertise on the Oculus and should spend ample time familiarizing themselves with the games or VR experiences they plan on using in the program.
- VR is still a brand-new technology to many of the patrons who come to VR programs, and staff must be prepared to demonstrate the technology competently, answer many questions, and repeat themselves. Staff should take on a training or teaching disposition since staff is teaching the program participant how to use the new equipment from the ground up. VR is actually very hands-on, especially when getting beginners started!

- Create posters or handouts that list the functions of the buttons on the controllers as well as some basic commands inside of the VR games/ experiences.
- Connect and work with an outside organization that specializes in working with the fifty-plus demographic. Organizations could include a local senior center, recreation facility, Senior Corp, VA/VFW, county or city committees on aging, and the like. Not only will working with an outside organization help you target your program marketing toward this age group in places they are likely to see it, but it will also add a layer of familiarity to individuals who otherwise would not think of attending a technology program at the library.
- If the program is to be off-site, scout the location a minimum of three months in advance. This is where collaborating with an outside organization that caters to the fifty-plus demographic is key. When scouting a

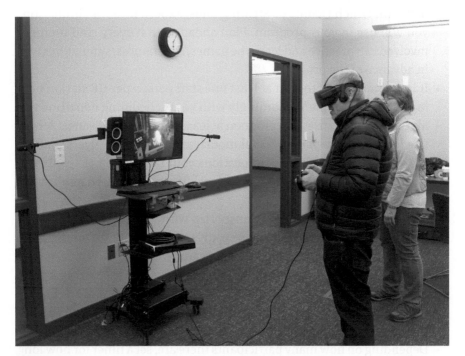

FIGURE 32.2 Library aide assists participant at a 55+ virtual reality event with Loveland Public Library; event was cosponsored and advertised by the Loveland Chilson Senior Center to engage with Loveland's senior community.

location, keep in mind space occupancy, seating, power outlets, lighting, outside interference, and internet access should last-minute updates be needed.

- Smaller groups are better for fifty-plus VR events; consider hosting a greater number of events for shorter durations of time versus a longer, larger event. This will limit the length of time people will have to wait and be less intimidating for incoming participants. Think about what your participants will do as they wait for their turn on the VR cart. Having additional video games to play, multiple VR carts available, or the gameplay visible on a projector screen will help those waiting stay interested and engaged.

Program Instructions

- Working with your partner organization, solidify the dates, times, and location that your program will take place.
- Settle on which Oculus or Steam games, experiences, or simulations you will use in your program. Plan ahead so that every staff member involved can practice and learn the games/experiences/simulations well in advance of the program.
- It is recommended to allot at least one staff person per VR station or at least two overall; plan accordingly with your scheduling department.
- Market and advertise your program at least six weeks in advance. Advertise in the newspaper, on social media, and with paper flyers that are more likely to be picked up at locations your targeted participants will frequent. Consider advertising in a local fifty-plus-focused publication or local magazine.
- Mobile VR carts can be easily transported without having to break them down, but should you need to do so, give yourself enough time to reassemble and test your equipment before the event.
- Set up the room a minimum of one hour in advance. Setting up the virtual space is important for accuracy with the Oculus sensors. Ensure that there is plenty of open space for participants to walk around without tripping or bumping into something.
- Depending on how many participants there are, set a timer for how long each person's turn can be. Timed gameplay can be turned on in Oculus' Demo Mode.

- As participants enter the event, set expectations regarding what they will be doing in the program and talk about VR and its uses; participants may want to discuss why VR is being offered by the library, how it affects them, or how they can relate.
- Be prepared to demonstrate the VR headset and controllers. When assisting the participants in putting on the headset and controllers for the first time, it is helpful to give step-by-step instructions and show them functions before instructing them on how to put on the headset. Help familiarize the participant with what they will see and/or do inside of the game/video/simulation.
- When it is a participant's turn, explain the different VR experiences they can choose from and allow them to pick the one that seems the most interesting. Have a specific VR experience in mind for absolute beginners and direct them toward it or let them choose between two to three options if they are unsure.
- Have participants use hand sanitizer before using the controllers. This prevents any residue build-up from blocking the sensors and ensures the controllers remain hygienic for other users.
- Try to avoid touching the participant if possible. If you must help the participant adjust the headset or get a grip on the controllers, give commands; if you absolutely must touch them, ask their permission first and explain what you are doing. For example, you could say, "I am going to untangle the controller from your left wrist."
- Check in with the participant during their VR experience to assess if they are having any negative effects. Offer a chair or fatigue mat. Vision or equilibrium issues can cause dizziness and disorientation for some, so keeping tabs on their comfort level will help prevent any catastrophes or potential health issues.
- Consider changing the experience/simulation/game/video to something different if you gauge that your participant is struggling or not having a good time. You can fall back on observational videos or VR experiences with limited movements if you find that your participant is having difficulty.
- Offer water or a snack after a participant's turn to ease them back into "reality." Ask them what they liked or didn't like about the experience. This will help you assess down the road what games/simulations/experiences are better than others, what is successful, and what may need tweaking.

- For those able to take multiple turns on the VR station, offer suggestions on which other VR experiences they would like to try.
- Encourage them to return to any future events.
- After the event, sanitize and breakdown the equipment to transport back to its storage or home location.
- Debrief with your staff and representatives from partner organizations to discuss how the event went, any mishaps, or any changes you might make at future events.

RECOMMENDED NEXT PROJECTS

If you find that your participants were thoroughly engaged, recommended next projects could look like:

- A themed event where all VR experiences, tours, games, or experiences are centered around a certain topic such as space or nature
- A mobile event during which the VR experience is taken to new locations such as a local business, club, or assisted living facility

If you have trouble getting this program off the ground or if your participants are disinterested, try reconsidering when/where your program is held or how it was advertised.

- Hosting a program at the time and place most comfortable for your specific targeted age group will increase the likelihood they will participate. Similarly, advertising the program in terms of virtual "experiences" and "simulations" that are relatable to them instead of as a "gaming" event may be more successful.
- You can also consider hosting this program in conjunction with another fifty-plus-targeted program or as part of a larger event that attracts adults. For example, a themed holiday event or local business event with multiple booths may be the perfect place to set up a VR tour or video.

Index

Y

Z